RAISING YOUR CHILD,
NOT BY FORCE BUT BY LOVE

RAISING YOUR CHILD, NOT BY FORCE BUT BY LOVE

by SIDNEY D. CRAIG

THE WESTMINSTER PRESS
Philadelphia

PUBLISHED BY THE WESTMINSTER PRESS ®
PHILADELPHIA, PENNSYLVANIA

PRINTED IN THE UNITED STATES OF AMERICA

Library of Congress Cataloging in Publication Data

Craig, Sidney D., 1927-
  Raising your child, not by force but by love.

  Bibliography: p.
  1. Children—Management. 2. Love. I. Title.
[DNLM: 1. Child psychology—Popular works. 2. Child rearing—Popular works. WS 105 C886r 1973]
HQ769.C915   649′.1   72-10436
ISBN 0-664-20956-4

To my beloved wife, Anita, whose unlimited patience and kindness served as the daily inspiration for a book about love. And to my beloved children, Constance Allison and Claudia Victoria, whose warmth, charm, and goodness of character reveal everything that is noble and beautiful about young people.

CONTENTS

ACKNOWLEDGMENTS

The writer wishes to express his most sincere appreciation to Dr. Roland W. Tapp for the many reasonable and objective suggestions that helped so greatly in the preparation of this manuscript.

I should also like to express my very deep feelings of affection and gratitude to those people who have permitted me to share in their lives as therapist or counselor. What they revealed of themselves enabled me to understand the wholesomeness and dignity of human beings.

INTRODUCTION

Many parents today are experiencing the sorrow of finding that their children become emotionally separated from them as the children approach young adulthood. These parents become concerned and disheartened as they observe their sons and daughters turning away from long-cherished parental values and toward various radical doctrines that seem both senseless and immoral. In many instances the rejection of parental values by the young is of such magnitude that the two generations can barely speak together without creating severe mutual antagonism. Family life in such situations is beset by constant quarreling and ill feelings in spite of the desire by all participants to live together in peace and harmony. A great many families have struggled to resolve this problem in a constructive manner. However, the ever-increasing number of young people from good homes who are dropping out of school, running away from home, or turning to the use of dangerous drugs attests to the difficulty of finding an effective solution. Many parents have already despaired of ever finding one.

But my own experience with numerous families does not support such a pessimistic view of the situation. I have found that there does exist a reliable set of principles that can guide parents in their efforts to reduce tension and conflict within the home. These principles have demonstrated their worth during thousands of years of mankind's recorded history. Because of

their proven dependability, I feel reasonably secure in offering parents the basis for hope implied in the following statement: There is no necessity for your child to become remote from you, to turn away from your most respected values, or to turn to the use of dangerous drugs—if you have the courage to act toward him in a manner consistent with those compassionate, humanitarian principles which you have learned from your own Judeo-Christian religious training.

There are several ideas implied in this brief statement which you may or may not accept as yet, but of which I hope to convince you. First, I am suggesting that whether or not your child turns away from parental values during his adolescence depends upon you, the parents, more than upon any other single factor. Specifically, it depends upon how you act toward him both before and during the time he is a teen-ager.

Secondly, I am suggesting that there exists both a correct and an incorrect way of dealing with the growing child, and that the correct way has already been identified and described for those parents who wish to use it.

Finally, I am suggesting that the Judeo-Christian religious tradition, as defined in the writings of the Old and the New Testament, provides the necessary and correct guidelines for parental behavior toward children which can prevent their turning away from the parents and toward drug use. Twentieth-century dynamic psychology and psychiatry can provide parents with identical principles stated in the more contemporary, scientific language appropriate for our times. However, the actual principles by which one human being can influence another to grow or develop in a psychologically healthy manner have been known for thousands of years.

In order for you to understand why these things are so, there are several important characteristics or principles of human nature and the social context in which it develops with which you must become familiar.

In the following chapters I will describe these principles for you individually and then show how they interact with one another to produce teen-age problems. On the basis of your understanding of these principles, you should be able to see why it is that parents play such an important role in determining the delinquent or nondelinquent nature of their children's behavior; and, also, I hope it will become obvious to you that a sensible solution to the problem of delinquency exists if parents have the courage to draw on their own religious heritage. Furthermore, it will become obvious why it is that the most conscientious parents are among those most likely to produce delinquency in their children.

For 1st SUN - EACH COUPLE Bring A List OF TEN (10) Problems AND A LIST OF 5 EXCUSES or REASONS FOR MisBehavior, AND 3 or 5 SOLUTIONS/REMEDIES or MOM/DAD'S REACTIONS - ADVICE.

WHAT WAS YOUR Biggest PARENT/CHILD Problem THIS WEEK - How DID you Resolve or SoLve iT? WHO WON! WAS A XTN value/Precept IN THE Solution? DID you ReDeem your ANGER?

1

THE RELATIONSHIP BETWEEN FEELINGS AND BEHAVIOR

Feelings play a crucial role in determining human behavior. Our behavior toward other persons is determined by our feelings toward them. Obviously, we behave differently toward those we like than toward those we dislike.

Assuming that we have no reason to hide or disguise our feelings, if we like certain people (feelings), we are more likely to spend time with them, talk with them, confide in them, do nice things for them, and in general we strive to make them happy. On the other hand, if we dislike or are angry with certain other people (feelings), we are likely to avoid spending time with them, avoid talking with them, avoid doing nice things for them, and in general we do not strive to make them happy. If sufficiently angered, we may even do things to hurt the other person.

Consider for a moment the case of a young man who wants a certain young woman to marry him. His problem is to determine how he should act so as to produce a specific feeling in her. If he chooses his behavior carefully (i.e., taking the girl to nice places, flattering her, being considerate and attentive, etc.), at some point during the relationship the woman will say to herself: "Oh, I really love that man. I think I'll marry him." In response to the feeling the man induced in her, the woman behaved as he wished. There is an important principle revealed in this couple's interaction: Loving feelings produce loving behavior.

This principle acts also in the production of negative feelings. Suppose, for example, that after this couple marries, the husband becomes less sensitive to his wife's needs. He no longer says complimentary things to her. He ignores her birthday, Valentine's Day, and their anniversary, and he begins spending his evenings away from home in the company of his boyhood friends. Gradually, the feelings of love in the wife will be converted to anger. Reflecting this anger, her behavior toward the husband will change. She may begin to scold a great deal, to become less affectionate and less sexually responsive. If sufficiently angered, she may sever the relationship entirely by divorce. The behavior of this young couple from courtship through divorce illustrates the operation of a significant law that governs interpersonal relationships: Loving feelings produce loving behavior. Angry feelings produce angry behavior. This is a law of human nature as predictable and inevitable as any of the laws that govern the physical universe.

This law is highly significant for parents because it operates in parent-child relationships as forcefully as in all others. If we want our children to spend time with us, to like us, to confide in us, to value some of the things we value, and to try to make us happy (for example, by their refraining from the use of dangerous drugs), we must behave toward them in ways that create feelings of love toward us rather than of dislike or anger. We cannot reasonably expect to receive "good" behavior from our children unless we create "good" feelings in them. Parents cannot create angry feelings in a child over a period of many years and then expect that the child will show loving behavior in return.

The key to understanding human behavior lies in understanding the feelings that underlie and produce the behavior. The key to guiding children's behavior into socially desirable channels consists in knowing how to create in the child those positive, loving feelings which will produce positive, loving, and, therefore, nondelinquent behavior. Or, conversely, the key lies in the parents' avoiding the production, cumulatively, of those angry feelings in the child which will produce angry, negativistic, delinquent behavior.

Unfortunately nature has introduced several factors into the parent-child relationship that make it extremely difficult for even the most sincere, well-meaning parent to convey to the child his true, loving feelings. The first of these is the complex nature of love itself.

Love is experienced in two different ways: (1) as an inner feeling or sensation and (2) as a series of overt actions. The person who is "in love" is aware of certain feelings or sensations taking place entirely within his own body. These feelings as such cannot be communicated to another person, except through some form of overt action. The person who is loved can know it or feel it only as he is the recipient of certain loving actions toward him on the part of the individual who is "in love."

Unfortunately, in the human species there is no instinctive or otherwise inevitable connection or relationship between the inner feeling of love and the kinds of overt actions that demonstrate the love. This means that it is entirely possible for a parent to love a child totally, inwardly, and yet to act toward that child in ways which do not reveal his love.

It happens very often that parents who are genuinely loving in their inner feelings for a child have by a misguided selection of actions conveyed to the child the message that he was not loved. Informing the child verbally of the parents' inner feelings and hugging and kissing him are usually insufficient to overcome the child's response to other long-term parental actions. Those parents with whom I have worked over the years have always been able to state honestly that they loved their children. Their children, however, had not experienced them as loving parents, because the children were responding to the parental actions and not to the inner feelings or intent.

Many parents, when they first come in for counseling regarding their children, are somewhat angry with psychologists and clergymen. They say things such as: "You have always told us that if we just loved them, they would be all right. Well, we do love them—and they're not all right. They even say they hate us. Why?" Their problem, of course, was not that they had failed to love their children but that they had failed to choose correctly those forms of behavior by which their inner feelings of love could have been revealed to the child. Very often I have said to such parents, "You know that you love your child and I know, but he doesn't know it." Counseling with such parents does not consist in urging the parents to love their own children. Rather, it consists in helping the parents to discover which forms of behavior may best reveal to the child what the parents felt toward him from the beginning.

The basic purpose of this book is to help people to select more carefully among the range of possible parental actions those which may communicate most effectively their true feelings to their children.

The second factor that nature has introduced which disrupts the parent-child relationship is prolonged childhood incompetence and dependency. The human being experiences the longest period of transition between the state of complete helplessness and the capacity for independent functioning of any known species. As you know, at birth and for a long period thereafter, the human infant is completely incompetent, unable to act effectively in any way to provide for his own welfare or safety. If left unsupervised, he would die. He possesses none of the instinctive, self-protective patterns of behavior that subhuman creatures develop very quickly in order to guarantee survival.

Almost everything the human being must know about surviving in the world and living in a civilized society must be learned. And it is the parents acting as agents of society as a whole who must both protect the child so that he survives and teach him the numerous attitudes, values, and complex forms of behavior demanded by the broader society. The parent is not only the primary guardian but also the primary teacher of the child.

Think for a moment of the extent of the parents' power over the child. During a crucial period of the child's lifetime, he will remain almost totally dependent on the decisions made by his parents as to whether or not his needs and desires are to be either gratified or denied. Although in certain limited areas the child in later years may be able to gratify himself, he will rarely, if ever, hold the power to satisfy his needs in the face of parental opposition, except surreptitiously.

From the very beginning, then, it is the parents who will determine when, how much, and what the child shall eat, when the child shall be awakened and when put to bed, how long and with whom he shall play, which possessions he shall or shall not have, how he shall dress, when he shall have haircuts, when, if a girl, she shall begin to wear lipstick, how long her skirts shall be, when she shall be permitted to associate with boys, go to parties, etc. This list could be extended endlessly, but to belabor this obvious point would be futile.

The important fact is that it is primarily the parents who hold and exercise this enormous power to determine the amount of pleasure or discomfort (or pain) the child will experience during his most formative, most impressionable, and, as I will describe shortly, least rational years.

It is because parents hold this power to determine pleasure or pain that they become objects of strong feelings from the child. For the child, especially the young child, "the world" is experienced primarily through contact with the parents. To the extent that the demands of the world are frustrating, the child will experience the parents as being frustrating. The same relationship would hold true concerning the child's experiencing of pleasure.

If you reflect for a moment, I am sure you will agree that most of the demands of the real world, both physical and social, are restrictive, coercive, inhibiting, or frustrating. There are far more "no-no's" than "yes-yes's." The child must not run into the street; he must not touch the hot stove, the glassware, the knickknacks on the coffee table. He must not eat too many sweets. He must kiss Aunt Agatha. He must sit up straight and chew with his mouth closed, etc. This means that in attempting to carry out their responsibilities in their socially prescribed role as parents, the vast majority of the time, necessarily, parents will have to use their authority to deny the child something he desires to do or to force him to do something he does not really wish to do. Parents, of course, have not solicited this authority or responsibility. Life has thrust it upon them. But the net effect is that, because of the dangers of the real world and the complexity of a civilized society, parents must frustrate their children endlessly while the children are growing up. Such frustration, of course, always has some impact on the person being frustrated.

In order for you to grasp the destructive impact of such frustration, there is another principle of the child's inherent way of reacting of which you should become aware. This is the factor of prolonged childhood irrationality. Recognition of the operation of this principle should enable you to see why it is that children often react so poorly, so perversely, to parental efforts to protect and raise them properly.

During all the child's years of growth, his thought processes and emotional reactions will operate in accordance with the following rule:

> Whenever a parent (or any other person in authority) acts so as to block the gratification of a child's immediate impulse or desire, the child will react with some degree of anger. This angry reaction will occur, regardless of the sense or lack of sense of the child's impulse.

For example, even if a parent stopped a young child from suddenly running into a busy thoroughfare, the child would feel some degree of anger toward the parent. "Ridiculous," you say. "The child has no right to react that way. It doesn't make sense. He has to learn that he can't do everything he wants to just because he wants to do it. Why, he could kill himself. What kind of world would this be if everyone did whatever he wanted to whenever he wanted to do it? He'll have to learn just like the rest of us!"

Logically, intellectually, rationally, and from a mature adult point of view you are correct on every point. Particularly, it is correct to define the child's reaction as completely irrational. But the fact that sensible adults agree that the child's response is self-destructive, uncivilized, indefensible, and irrational will not make it any less real. No matter how forcefully we disapprove of this characteristic of a child's reaction pattern, we must recognize it as a recurring event of childhood with which we must learn to deal. Acknowledging the existence of this type of reaction does not imply adult approval. But in the same sense that scientists study destructive germs in order to be able to protect human life, we must be willing to study these undesirable behavioral characteristics in order to protect our children.

My experience has shown that the parents' failure to recognize the existence of childhood irrationality permits them to make significant errors in dealing with their children. Since parents cannot believe that children will get angry when they have no logical reason to do so, when what the parents are doing is for the child's own good, they persist in their well-meaning actions. Then they are amazed at the amount of logically unjustified anger that has built up gradually to explosive proportions in their own children. It is the child's misunderstanding of his parents' feelings and motives that produces the animosity the child feels toward the parents. This misunderstanding in turn generates various forms of nonloving behavior.

To summarize what I have tried to present in this chapter: (1) The long-term incompetence of the child and his dependence on the parents gives them extensive power to control the degree of pleasure (gratification) or pain (frustration) the child will experience during his formative years. (2) The demands of physical reality (i.e., Fire burns) and a complex social system (i.e., You must take turns) make it necessary for the parents, in fulfilling their responsibility to their children and to society, to frustrate their children repeatedly. (3) It is an inevitable although irrational characteristic of the child's nature that whenever one of his immediate needs, impulses, wishes, or desires is blocked or frustrated, he will experience some degree of anger toward the person doing the frustrating. (4) Since the responsible parent must necessarily frustrate his child's impulses on a monumental scale while the child is growing up, it is inevitable that the child will experience a significant and even pathological degree of anger toward his parents.

Paradoxically, it is the most conscientious, dependable, and highly organized parents who are likely to have the angriest children, because they are more fully aware of and dedicated to fulfilling their responsibilities to their own children and to society. In doing what they consider to be their normal parental duty, these conscientious parents inadvertently but repeatedly block, thwart, and frustrate their child's needs and desires. This creates a great intensity of anger in the child. As I have already indicated, it is the angry child who is most likely to turn away from his family and toward delinquent behavior as a means of expressing his anger.

2

THE ROLE OF IRRATIONAL CHILDHOOD THINKING

You have had a brief glimpse of irrational thinking in our discussion of the child's inevitable angry reaction to having an impulse or a desire thwarted. As you will see, childhood irrationality is probably the most important single factor acting to distort and disrupt the parents' efforts to establish a close, loving relationship with their children.

Irrational thinking is a defective mode of thinking which produces unsound, useless, and even self-destructive solutions to everyday problems. It evades, distorts, and even completely reverses the rules of common sense and logic which mankind has found over the centuries to be worthwhile and dependable.

Any adult who has ever associated with children knows from painful experience how irrational a child's thinking can be. Nevertheless, few adults are aware of the nature and the extent of childhood irrationality. Fewer still are able to deal with it constructively, so as to reinforce rather than disrupt the parent-child relationship.

A description of the three irrational mechanisms most commonly displayed by children is presented here.

1. *Narcissism.* Children are born in a state of total narcissism. This absolute narcissism decreases slightly each year. However, during most of his childhood, the child will remain largely, if not overwhelmingly, narcissistic. Children care exclusively about the gratification of their own needs and impulses. They

may be aware that there are other people in the world besides themselves, but they have no interest or desire in seeing that the needs or desires of these other people are taken care of. So far as the child is concerned, these other people are no more important and are entitled to no greater degree of consideration than is given inanimate objects.

When the child is very young, he is not even aware that other people have feelings. The infant may giggle while scratching his mother's face until it bleeds. He may step on her face without hesitation if he is "heading" for a toy and her face is in the way. When the child is somewhat older, he may become aware that other people do have feelings, but he doesn't consider this fact important enough to let it affect his behavior toward them. In later childhood, the narcissistic view of the world may be revealed when the child makes remarks such as, "Mommy, if you died, who would cook for me?" During the teen-age years, the narcissism is shown, typically, in the young teen-ager making excessive demands on an already overworked and probably tired parent. As an example of this, a teen-ager who has spent her day lounging at the beach and then reclining in front of the television set may suddenly demand that her mother, who has been working all day, iron a fancy dress which the girl is quite capable of ironing herself.

One way of understanding the nature of childhood narcissism would be as follows: The child considers that his fair share of what life has to offer consists of 100 percent of what is available. If the child receives less than 100 percent, he is going to resent it. Therefore, he will resent anyone or anything that distracts from the 100-percent satisfaction of his needs. Inevitably, then, he will resent any and all siblings. He will resent other children with whom he is forced to share anything. He will resent family pets if they are getting some portion of his parents' attention that he wants. Very young children will even attempt to tear up a newspaper the mother might be reading if the child wants her attention.

This insatiable narcissism creates recurring problems for parents with more than one child. No matter how fairly the parents attempt to divide their attention and affection equally between two or more children, each child will feel cheated and angry because he has received less than 100 percent. Quarreling, bickering, and fighting between siblings is inevitable. Moreover, whenever a parent intervenes on one side or the other, no matter how fair or just his intent and resulting decision, at least one of the children inevitably will feel cheated and abused and will become angry with the parent.

The following are a few examples of situations in which narcissism is operating that are so maddening for parents. A mother may buy two identical rubber balls, one for each of her two children. To the naked eye, and very likely under microscopic examination, both balls would appear identical. One or the other child, however, will be convinced that the other got the "better" ball and will be very unhappy. Nothing the parent can say will placate or reassure that child. Very likely, even if a trade could be arranged, the complaining child would want back the ball he originally had. There is no rational solution available to this problem since basically the child is unhappy because he does not have both balls. This is the only "solution" that would please him. This is impossible, of course, since there is a sibling with needs and feelings of his own who must be considered also. But the child in his natural state of narcissism will resent the necessity for any portion of the environment going to anyone other than himself.

One evening the parents have a nice idea. They decide to take their two children to a good movie. Enthused, the older brother asks permission to invite a friend. The parents agree. He telephones his friend but finds that the friend cannot go with him that evening. Meanwhile, his sister, who has been listening, gets the idea that she too would like to invite a friend. When she asks permission, the brother objects. He says it's unfair, she shouldn't ask a friend if his friend can't go. They should go to the movie "as a family." What began as a happy idea on the part of the parents for spending a pleasant evening with their children becomes a "big mess." Now they have one pouting, crying youngster sitting glaring, with arms folded, in the back of the car. They have had to scold him, calling him "selfish . . . ungrateful . . . a baby." Sister and her friend are smiling broadly all the while they enjoy brother's discomfort. He, in turn, is hating them in every way he can think of. Just wait till he gets hold of her at home, or on the way to school, etc.

At Christmastime, the parents are especially generous and spend a great deal of money to buy the child many of the things he wanted. One week after the holiday gift period, when a single request is denied, the child complains loudly, "You never buy me anything."

Cheating is another expression of the child's narcissism. In competitive games there is usually only one winner, and each child wants to be that one. Parents are often amazed at the lengths to which young children will go in order to win a "simple" game. They can't understand why children "won't play by the rules" or why it is that a child will enjoy winning even though the child knows he cheated. Again, winning is a reward that life can offer. The narcissistic child feels it is his right to have that particular reward. His need is so great that if life won't give it to him, he must find ways to get it, even if the way he chooses doesn't make sense by adult standards. We have all seen young children weeping bitterly, apparently broken-hearted, because they didn't win some (to us) insignificant prize at a birthday party.

"Me first" is the child's principal philosophy for a long time. What adult has not observed youngsters pushing and shoving in order to be first in line after a teacher or someone else in authority has told them to line up? Parents look on with horror when two, three, or more of their children yank open the door of the family car, each trying to get ahead of the others. Once inside the car, this primordial battle continues over who will sit next to the window, etc. It is an unhappy characteristic of human existence that every child is born with this instinctive need to be first in a world where obviously not everyone can be first.

You will see other examples of narcissism in the playground and schoolyard every day: the bigger children taking swings away from smaller ones; or holding equipment, not taking turns. Where there is no competing greater power, children show their basic impulses undisguised.

2. *Negativism.* Beginning at approximately age two and for at least five years thereafter, all children become markedly negativistic. At these early ages, the surest way to make a child run away from you is to give him a direct command to come to you. This behavior will persist in spite of the fact that he may be punished for it repeatedly.

Any parent who has lived through this period with a child could fill an encyclopedia-sized volume with everyday illustrations of such negativism. The following are just a few:

A father has been away for several days. He returns home and throws open his arms to give his five-year-old a gigantic hug and kiss. She runs away from him, or if he catches her and picks her up, she arches her back away from him. This, in spite of the fact that everyone knows that this child adores her father.

The mother lays out green shoes to go with an outfit the child will be wearing. Instantly, the child decides she wants to wear the red shoes. Similarly, on the warmest day of the year, the child will decide to wear the warmest dress she owns. Conversely, on the coolest day she will choose a sleeveless dress. This type of incident leaves mothers gnashing their teeth.

The classic illustration in this field, however, which all parents will recognize instantly, centers around the child's use of bowel and bladder movements. Before taking a young child to a place where it would be inconvenient for him to urinate, most parents will urge him to use the toilet. Almost invariably, the child will say he doesn't "have to go" at that convenient time. But in the middle of a church service, at a ball game, on a freeway, or as soon as hot food is served in a restaurant, the child will certainly "have to go now." Often at such times, the child will have a very faint smirk on his face. Even though he can't control the negativism, he is aware of the effect it has on the parents.

3. *Guilt resistance*. Very early in life children develop incredibly sophisticated devices for avoiding any sense of personal responsibility or guilt for their own impulsive, unwise, or antisocial actions.

Children hate to admit that they have done anything wrong. Even youngsters who cannot yet speak clearly are knowledgeable enough to point their fingers toward the nearest sibling or playmate and say, "ee d'it," in order to avoid blame. The child learns to do this in the beginning as a way of evading punishment. Eventually, however, wrongdoing produces an inner sensation or feeling of guilt which is, itself, extremely unpleasant or even painful. In order to avoid this painful inner feeling, the child will go to extraordinary lengths. Some means of escaping such guilt feelings appear quite irrational to adults, yet they fulfill the child's needs.

Let us examine some of the mental mechanisms that children use to evade punishment or guilt:

a. Children lie. A child will routinely answer "No" to all the following questions: "Did you take the last cookie? Did you hit your brother? Did you throw dirt over the fence? Did you hear me calling you?"

b. Children will distort and deny obvious reality. Even when the child is caught red-handed in the midst of some wrongful act he will deny his guilt. Adults are often astonished at the tenacity with which the child will persist in denying his guilt even in the face of the threat of increased punishment for lying. The more rational adult has difficulty in accepting the fact that the child could tolerate the punishment to be administered far more comfortably than he could the pain of public and inner acknowledgment of his own guilt.

c. Children rationalize. When caught in some form of misbehavior, children will find a logical-sounding reason for it which absolves them of responsibility. This trait is as old as mankind's history. Adam blamed Eve for giving him the apple, and Eve blamed the snake. Another commonly heard rationalization is, "Well, they were all doing it." The typical parental response, "If they were all jumping off a bridge, would you have to jump off also?" does not register with the child.

Sometimes this rationalizing takes the form of the child's using, in some absurd way, a virtue that the parent has taught which makes sense when used in moderation. For example, a mother might be attempting to discourage her thirteen-year-old daughter from associating with a girl who has been expelled from school, is sexually promiscuous, and is known to be a chronic drug user. In order to deny the sense of the parent's request, the child will reply, "Mother, you always taught me not to reject people just because they were different from us."

Often the rationalizing takes on a distinct paranoid quality. In one instance that I am aware of, a little boy had stolen a baseball that belonged to a friend of his. When asked about this by his father, the child replied: "I only did it to teach Jimmie a lesson. He left that baseball on his front porch for a week just to tempt me!"

More commonly, the child reveals the paranoid quality in this manner: He forgets his sweater at the playground. When he returns home and realizes what he has done, the child begins crying and yelling at his mother for making him lose it.

I want to emphasize that all the illustrations given of irrational thinking, including those which follow immediately below, are responses given by normal children during the course of routine daily interaction with their parents.

d. Children can reverse mentally the order in which events occurred. This mechanism is actually a combination of several others. Partly it is rationalizing. Partly it reflects selective forgetting, partly it is blaming others, and in some part it is the denial of reality. This characteristic has enormous impact on the course of parent-child relationships because of its intimate relationship with punishment. It is the mechanism that the child uses most commonly to deal with punishment in such a way as to evade guilt. As you shall see, the use of this irrational mechanism by the child inhibits the healthy growth of conscience and ultimately, therefore, blocks the capacity for self-control. What replaces the healthy guilt is hostility toward the parents which serves to inhibit further the growth of conscience and self-control.

The process occurs in this way: First, the child does something wrong. Let's say that he returns home at six thirty in the evening instead of at five o'clock as he had been instructed. The mother decides that he should be punished in order to teach him a lesson. Therefore, after dinner, he is sent to his room and forbidden to watch television for that evening. The parent is hoping that the child, sitting alone in his room, is thinking: Gee, I guess I was bad today. I came home late and I didn't even telephone my mother. Now I'm being punished for what I did. I guess I shouldn't be bad anymore.

If the child were a rational creature, he would undoubtedly be thinking along these lines and the punishment would be fulfilling the parent's objective. Unfortunately, however, the child's thinking would sound a lot more like this: No wonder I come home late. She's always bugging me. Anyone with a mother like that would come home late. Who wants to come home to a house like this where they sit you in your room and you can't even have any fun?

In the case of the child who returned home late for dinner, the parent was hoping that the punishment applied would lead to his doing a good deal of thinking about himself. In the illustration of his thought processes as the parent visualized them, the word "I" appeared very frequently. The parent's own rational way of thinking, supported by other sources of rational information in our society, encourages the parent's unrealistic belief that this is actually what takes place in the child's mind. Some of the very best television shows that present a series involving a family convey such misinformation repeatedly. Who among us has not seen the kindly television father call his erring son before him and with a kind but reproving expression send the son to his room to "think things over"? The son always returns contrite and makes amends for whatever wrong he has done. Partly through such influences, parents come to believe that this is a useful model of parental behavior and a realistic

approximation of childhood thinking which they might reasonably expect to occur in their own families.

This is simply impossible. Because of the child's strong desire to evade guilt, he will use all sorts of devices to justify his own actions and find fault with someone other than himself. The second example I gave of the child's thoughts is much more typical. In that example, you could observe that most or all of his criticism was being directed against the mother rather than at himself.

Because of the child's ability to reverse cause-and-effect sequences in his mind, what should be an intrapsychic conflict—that is, a struggle within the child between his good impulses and his bad impulses—becomes instead an interpersonal conflict between the child and his mother. Since the primary goal of the child in such situations is to evade guilt rather than "to learn from experience," the parent must be cast in the role of villain, and the child in the role of the innocent victim of persecution. Once the child has redefined the situation in this manner, he feels that he is entitled to sympathy and understanding and not (in his mind) unjust punishment.

In such situations, that portion of the child's feeling and thought processes which might have operated to produce self-control and good behavior does not develop. Rather, standards of conduct are seen by the child as something external to himself which reside in and are the property of the parent. Since the child has already decided, irrationally, that he is the innocent victim of parental persecution, he feels no need to develop any loyalty to the parental standards. To him such standards represent nothing more than the constant threat of guilt, which he tries to evade.

Because of the child's irrationality, the use of punishment as a deterrent or as a teaching device, no matter how well meant by the parent, provides the child with the "ammunition" he needs to justify with a minimum of guilt his own continuing misbehavior.

Once the child has begun to distort his perception of his own and the parents' roles and responsibilities regarding his being punished, the possibilities for adequate growth of conscience within the child are radically reduced. The child's irrationality will interact with the parental use of punishment or disapproval so as to interfere with the development of those aspects of the child's mental functioning which we refer to as conscience. Contrary to the parents' desire in using punishment as a teaching device, good behavior will not become the child's primary goal. Rather, the child's goals will become those of: (1) maintaining his image of himself as the "good guy" and the parents as the evil persecutors; (2) avoiding getting caught in misbehavior by someone in authority; and (3) seeking out other like-minded children who will support and sustain his own image of himself as an innocent, persecuted individual.

You may be able to discern now why it is that childhood irrationality plays such a destructive role in the child's personality development and on the parent-child relationship. The child's irrational thought processes are the first link in a chain of events which produces, inevitably, angry feelings in the child. And, as I have indicated, angry feelings produce angry behavior.

The destructive situation unfolds in the following manner: Virtually all overt behavioral manifestations of the child's irrationality demand some form of response on the part of the parent which the child will resent because he is irrational. Such parental response may include restraint of some sort ("No, you can't stay up late tonight"), reprimands ("You should know better than to hit your brother"), disapproval ("I'm fed up with you and your selfishness"), punishment ("You won't leave this house for one week"), reminders ("Did you do your chores today?"), and general education ("Chew with your mouth closed"). The incredible dilemma posed for the parent is this— that the same irrational brain which first produced the undesirable behavior will then sit in judgment on the parents' efforts to deal with the original irrationally produced misconduct. There is an almost comical aspect to this situation. First, the irrational mind of the child produces some form of obviously unacceptable behavior, behavior that might even be extremely dangerous to the child. Then having generated the defective behavior, it is the same irrational child-mind that must evaluate and respond to the parents' efforts to modify or eliminate the irrational behavior. It is the parents' lack of awareness of the irrational interpreter of their actions that permits them, the parents, to make the same mistakes generation after generation, thus producing unwholesome degrees of anger in their children.

The most commonly used and socially acceptable parental response to a display of irrational behavior (a temper tantrum, for example) is to punish the child for it. Most parents operate according to the widely held belief that the child will not repeat a form of behavior for which he has been administered a dose of pain. This technique has a kind of surface validity, because very often in the face of repeated punishment and threats of punishment a child will abandon a particular form of behavior. When the offensive form of behavior diminishes in frequency, the parent is reassured that he is following the proper philosophy and fulfilling his duty both to the child and to the broader society.

But unfortunately the problem is more complex. Just as we saw in the earlier discussion of love, irrationality too has an inner, experiential, unobservable quality as well as an outer, observable behavioral manifestation.

When the parent punishes the child, all that the child does is to eliminate the overt evidence of his irrational needs, desires, and way of thinking. Punishment does not change in any manner whatsoever the underlying irrational thought processes that produced the unacceptable behavior originally. The "badness" has merely gone underground.

When a parent depends to a great extent on disapproval and punishment as means to deal with the child's unacceptable behavior, a long-term process of building anger within the child takes place. Gradually and imperceptibly, over a period of years, the angry feelings are growing and competing with the loving feelings for control of the child's personality. The parent remains unaware that there is anything to be concerned about because outwardly, in response to properly administered punishment, the child is behaving dutifully and is gradually eliminating all the selfish, obnoxious, spoiled ways in which "poorly trained" children act. But after years in a "latency" period, the irrational anger that has been accumulating comes to outweigh the power of loving feelings to restrain them. When this occurs, the outward behavior of the child changes radically. A typical delinquent picture then emerges, reflecting the intense angry feelings "inside." Even at this point it cannot be said that the child does not love his parents. He still loves them and at times may act very lovingly. But the angry feelings predominate and determine the major portion of the child's behavior.

The change from good to bad behavior is often sudden, occurring most frequently when the child approaches adolescence. For this reason, parents are likely to blame the change on chance coincidences, not recognizing that they are witnessing the fruition of a lifelong process. Some parents review their own behavior and conclude that they had not been punitive enough, believing that if they had just been tougher, they would have gained complete control over the child's bad impulses. And some people blame drugs, as if the use of drugs, rather than being symptomatic of a person "sick" with rage, had caused the child's behavior to change.

Parents who assess the situation in this manner are merely deceiving themselves. They are either unaware of or are refusing to recognize the long-term deterioration in their own relationship with the child caused in large measure by the operation of the child's irrational thinking. To punish the child severely at this point, such as by forbidding him to see a certain friend, only intensifies the child's irrational anger and makes the situation worse.

If parents can recognize and acknowledge the threat that irrationality presents to the parent-child relationship, they can take steps when the child is still young to protect the relationship. In several of the later chapters in this book I will outline steps that may be taken by parents to nullify the potentially destructive impact of childhood irrationality.

3

THE REAL DANGER
OF PERMISSIVENESS

People have never been surprised to find that many irresponsible, delinquent, drug-addicted, or otherwise troubled children have been raised in very poor home environments. This relationship between the "sick" home and the "sick" child has been known for centuries. It is entirely reasonable to expect, and repeated experience has confirmed, that children raised by parents who are morally defective, infantile, indolent, irresponsible, incompetent, or criminal should turn "bad." (Like father, like son.) We may infer safely that in such families the parents set a poor example, failed to teach proper ethical standards and paid insufficient attention to the child's physical and emotional needs. We may even suspect that such parents did not really want or love their children. Common sense tells us that problem children should arise within such a family context.

However, what has been extremely puzzling to parents for centuries is the problem of how to explain those "wild," irresponsible, delinquent children who were reared by parents believed to be honest, responsible, and hard-working citizens. This opposition between the parents' morality and that of the child has occurred so regularly throughout the period of man's recorded history that it has become part of our folklore. Numerous novels and stage plays center around a prominent person whose son becomes the town's ne'er-do-well or the clergyman's daughter who becomes the town harlot.

Historically, in their attempts to explain this phenomenon, the public has utilized three major theories. The oldest of the three held that the bad child had been possessed by the devil or some other evil spirit. Common sense then dictated that the proper course of action to cure the condition was to "beat the devil" out of the child. As mankind turned away from this primitive demonology, a new idea more compatible with modern, scientific thinking developed. This was the theory of the hereditary transmission of behavioral or personality traits. According to this theory, if a "bad" child suddenly showed up in the middle of a "good" family, it was suspected that one of his ancestors had possessed a defective gene. Presumably then, this gene suddenly manifested itself in the child who was the carrier of the "bad seed." Gradually this idea, too, came to be discredited by twentieth-century geneticists, biologists, and psychologists. There remained, then, but one widely accepted explanation for this phenomenon which has not been refuted by more advanced thinking.

This third explanation places the blame for delinquent children on permissive treatment by the parents. This theory has always coexisted with the other two. But now, since the other two theories have passed from the scene, this one has emerged as the overwhelming favorite.

Specifically, according to this explanation, the parents of delinquent children have been either too ignorant or too irresponsible to have punished their children for various of the child's minor and major transgressions. Accordingly, it is the parents' failure or refusal to have used firm, fair, consistent, and even harsh punishment that permitted the child to develop a wild, irresponsible, or antisocial pattern of behavior. Since, according to this theory, the parents' aversion to using punishment as a restraining force permitted the child to develop his delinquent pattern, this particular form of parental failure is known today as permissiveness.

As I said previously, this explanation which holds the parents to blame is no less ancient than the demonic and hereditary theories that it has survived. The fact that it is labeled with the rather contemporary-sounding word "permissiveness" merely disguises its antiquity. Its roots, however, can be clearly seen in admonitions to parents such as, "As the twig is bent, so grows the tree," and "He who hates not his child, spares not the rod."

Currently, then, warnings against parental permissiveness represent the major theoretical guideline available to parents and responsible authorities in their efforts to understand, prevent, and treat behavioral disorders, including prominently today the excessive use of dangerous drugs.

I hope to convince you that permissiveness should not be accepted as a valid explanation for what is wrong with large numbers of young people today. This is not to defend or condone permissiveness. To the extent that it is practiced it would have a detrimental effect on a child's personality. However, my own experience with a great many families has convinced me that there are very few people in this country sufficiently remote from the mainstream of information available as to have remained uninformed concerning the dangers of genuine permissiveness. Such information is provided daily in massive amounts through churches and school systems, through the courts and law-enforcement agencies, through government-sponsored education programs, and directly and indirectly through all the forms of the mass media. The dangers of permissiveness are described in full-length books, in magazine articles, in the advice columns of daily newspapers, and in pamphlets produced by public-spirited citizens. The majority, popularly held viewpoint is presented almost universally as the most valid model for parents to follow.

At one time during the course of my work as a psychologist I was employed by an institution that provided custodial care and treatment for mentally ill patients. These people had been declared insane, and legally confined within a locked institution. In my talks with these patients, many of whom were parents, I found that they were acutely aware of the dangers of permissiveness in the raising of their own children. Years later I worked extensively with adults diagnosed as either borderline or mentally defective (I.Q.s of 65 and below). Most were eligible to receive financial aid from the state because of the severity of their intellectual deficit. These people, too, in their own inarticulate way, described to me repeatedly how careful they had to be in raising their children in order to avoid spoiling them.

It is unlikely that any subject in this country could produce such widespread agreement as that of the dangers to the child of parental permissiveness.

Yet, what I hope to convince the reader is that the "enemy" of the child is not permissiveness, but rather the fear of being permissive. It is this fear which drives good, middle-class American parents to behave toward their children in those callous, unsympathetic, insensitive ways which ultimately result in youthful delinquency. It is this fear of permissiveness which frightens parents away from demonstrating those humane, constructive, conciliatory forms of behavior which would enhance rather than destroy their relationship with their children. It is the parents' fear of permissiveness that forces them to abandon as the major child-rearing resource their own legitimate Judeo-Christian heritage which stresses gentleness, kindness, trust, faith, and forgiveness in one's relationship with others. Having been forced by an antiquated theory to abandon those forms of behavior which could produce loving feelings in their children, the parents must inevitably produce angry feelings with tragic consequences.

The new insight I am trying to present to the reader is that, contrary to what you may now believe, vast numbers of children who become delinquent and turn to the use of dangerous drugs have not been raised permissively. Nor do they come from homes in which the parents have been irresponsible, incompetent, or otherwise derelict in meeting their responsibilities to their children. Rather, these drug-using children have been reared by parents who are the most well-organized, highly informed, sincere, intelligent, dedicated, and responsible members of the community. It is the average, middle-class parent, being guided primarily by the fear of being permissive, who, during the normal process of responsible child-rearing, produces unknowingly a degree of hostile feelings in the child which in turn produces various forms of antisocial behavior.

For centuries people have been raising their children following the age-old theory that a sufficient degree of punishment judiciously applied would create good character and good behavior. Yet, as I have already indicated, the failures of this technique are so numerous that they have become enshrined in our literature. How does one account for the incredible longevity of this ancient theory in the face of massive, nonsupportive evidence? I should like to discuss several reasons with you in detail so that you will be better able to assess the usefulness of this fear-of-spoiling theory for your own children.

The primary reason for the persistence of public confidence in the effectiveness of punishment is that punishment does affect behavior and the results are almost immediate. Particularly when the child is young, punishment produces the immediately observable changes in behavior the parent desires. As any parent knows, if a young child's hand is slapped often enough and hard enough, the child will stop doing with that hand what the parent does not want him to do with it. This immediately observable cause-and-effect sequence gives the use of punishment the appearance of indisputable validity. The common sense of the parent inclines him to accept the evidence of his own senses. Thus, logic and common sense backed up by widespread social approval dictate that parents continue to depend on the theory that demands punishment for misbehavior rather than gamble on some more abstract theory which promises good behavior later but provides less immediately observable results in controlling the child's behavior here and now.

Let us look at a case history and see how the parents become increasingly confident that their technique of child-rearing is the correct one.

The parents were able to eliminate their child's tendency at age two and one half, to open certain cabinet doors by slapping his hands. (Punishment worked.) When he was three and one half, they were able to put a stop to his temper tantrums by spanking him. Occasionally, they used a long stick if the bare hand alone was insufficient. (Punishment worked.) When he was five years old, they put a stop to his using "dirty" words by washing his mouth with soap. (Punishment worked.) He presented no problem at the dinner table because he was punished if he showed poor manners. If he "ate like a pig" or refused to try new foods, or if he didn't finish all the food on his plate, he was sent to his room. (Again punishment worked.) At age nine the parents stopped his tendency to come home late for dinner by "grounding" him for one week each time he was late. Thus, all the child's behavior problems were "solved" by the consistent use of mild to moderate degrees of punishment.

Now "suddenly" at age thirteen, the child becomes apathetic and hostile. He does not work in class and is in constant conflict with school authorities. He uses foul language right to his mother's face. To culminate a sequence of minor delinquent actions, the child is caught "popping" pills in the lavatory at school.

What would any sensible parent believe was called for next? Obviously the same thing that had been successful in "solving" all the child's behavior problems during the preceding years. Only now, because of the seriousness of the child's misbehavior, a more severe punishment than had ever been used before would appear appropriate. In such a situation, the average, sincere, but now terribly alarmed parent might administer the most severe beating the child had ever received.

As you can see, the fact that punishment appeared to work successfully every time it was used makes it impossible for the parent to conceive of using any other technique. Thus, the immediately demonstrable effect of punishment has seduced generations of sensible adults into embracing it as the technique of choice in raising children.

The second factor that accounts for the longevity of this old approach is the overwhelming public belief in its effectiveness. This massive public belief in the usefulness of punishment is itself created by factor number one described above. However, once the nearly universal public acceptance is achieved, the public pressure itself becomes a factor that perpetuates the belief. The individual parent is hopelessly intimidated by the existence of a theory that historically and to the present has achieved the status of an unassailable virtue.

For the individual parent to deviate from this accepted dogma would have the same meaning and social consequences for him as if he had deviated from one of the Ten Commandments. First, of course, he would feel guilty because he would believe that he was contributing to the destruction of his own child. Secondly, for the individual parent to deviate from the accepted pattern would expose him to public rebuke, ridicule, and condemnation. The parent's belief in the correctness of what he is doing with the child reinforced by the massive societal approval for his actions makes it almost impossible for him to deal with the child in any other manner than is prescribed by the "Don't spoil 'em" approach.

Thus, the responsible parent is trapped by his conscience into alienating the child. But the theory itself maintains its aura of rightness. The blame, if things go wrong, ultimately comes to reside in the child, whose nervous system presumably was so defective that it would not respond correctly to the obviously correct system of discipline.

A third reason for continued public acceptance of the archaic theory is the ready availability of numerous rationalizations that explain away all failures of the theory to produce the desired results. It has proven extraordinarily difficult to discredit this theory because of these rationalizations. The proponents of this theory do not reassess its validity when it produces unwanted consequences. Rather, they seek to blame one of the participants involved in the situation, either the parents or the child, for failure to use it or failure to respond to it properly. These attempts to redistribute blame become so distorted at times that obvious failures of the theory are redefined as successes. If these obvious failures are viewed as successes, it is all but impossible to assess this theory with any degree of objectivity.

The foremost of these rationalizations takes the form of

blaming the parent for various deficiencies. The first deficiency attributed to the parent is that he was not sufficiently intelligent or informed to be aware of the dangers of permissiveness. The assumption is made, automatically, that whenever a child becomes delinquent the parent has raised him permissively. This is only an assumption, since there is usually no evidence whatsoever that the child was raised permissively. What is taken for "evidence" is the fact that the child is "in trouble." This type of reasoning is circular and logically indefensible.

This assessment of the situation is most likely to occur in those cases in which the parent of the delinquent child is a publicly known figure who is politically liberal and/or wealthy. The consensus of public opinion, then, is that the liberal parent raised his child permissively, consistent with his liberal political philosophy. The wealthy parent is presumed to have spoiled his child "rotten" by giving him "everything he ever wanted." Even in the absence of independent confirmatory evidence, liberals and wealthy people may find it very difficult to prove that they did not, in fact, spoil their children.

But with increasing frequency now, it has come to the attention of the public that many irresponsible, delinquent, drug-using, suicidal children come from homes in which the parents (even if wealthy) are known, unmistakably, to be responsible, civic-minded, and politically conservative. Such parents might include clergymen, physicians, law-enforcement officers, chiefs of police, judges, career military officers, conservative businessmen, politicians, and workingmen.

What do proponents of this theory do with the evidence that delinquent children come from homes in which the parents were obviously well informed as to the dangers of permissiveness and spoiling? One would hope that this would weaken the public's belief in the value of the theory. However, this does not occur. Rather, new rationalizations are introduced that vindicate the theory, but find fault with the parent. Now, since these parents have publicly embraced the virtuous theory so that it must be assumed that their children were not raised permissively, the excuse is offered that the parents themselves were defective people. The new position taken, then, is that the theory they used was correct but they were such nonvirtuous people that the theory could not produce its good results.

Thus, the public begins the intriguing but uncharitable search for flaws or defects in the parents' character. There are many variations of what the conservative parent may be accused of. Hypocrisy is currently the "in" word. The reasoning goes approximately like this: "Oh, yes, I know that Senator_____ (an ex-FBI man) would never have raised his child permissively, but you know politicians are all hypocrites. How else would you expect the son of a hypocrite to turn out?" (The parent might also be accused of having been covertly alcoholic, a swindler, and/or an adulterer.)

Who among us has not seen the final confrontation scene of the television drama in which the teen-age son, locked up in jail for drug use, snarls at his outwardly respectable father: "It's your fault. You've been playing around with your secretary for years." In another variation of this, the teen-ager blames both parents for his predicament—his mother uses prescription drugs for her headaches and his father spends too much time at the office. (The father's "sin" here is materialism.)

Such ideas, of course, find a receptive audience among young people who enjoy holding such fantasies of adults whom they both fear and envy. However, it is highly irresponsible for mature adults to present such distorted fantasies as if they represented sensible explanations for children's misbehavior.

The purpose of these rationalizations, encouraged and supported by public opinion and the mass media, is to demonstrate to the audience that the traditional theory is valid, but only when applied by virtuous parents. Even respected experts are sometimes guilty of this form of rationalization.

On April 5, 1971, *Time* magazine quoted Mr. Barr, the headmaster at Manhattan's private Dalton School, as follows: "The trouble with many children is that their fathers are mothers and their mothers are sisters." Apparently desperate to find any rationalization that would appear to support the old theory of parental incompetence, Mr. Barr would have us believe that paternal homosexuality is the significant factor in childhood delinquency.

The following statement appeared in *Time* magazine, August 17, 1970: "It is among many middle- and upper-class Americans that the estrangement of the young is strongest. . . . Parents who lose control of their children are usually confused about their own values and identities. Lacking authority, such parents cannot provide the key ingredient of growing up: a loving force to rebel against." The article continues, "Psychoanalyst Helene Deutsch believes that many parents themselves are still emotional adolescents and it is evident not only in their adoption of youthful dress and fads but in a lack of inner maturity as well."

And the noted authority on infant care, Dr. Spock, comments, "The delinquent child is often acting-out his parents' unconscious desires." [1] Thus, if you can't find an obvious flaw in the parents' personalities, search for one that is deeper—hidden and unconscious.

The message from these people is always the same: Our theory is correct. If it appears that it didn't produce the desired result, it must be someone else's fault. The parent didn't know about the evils of permissiveness. If he did know and the knowledge didn't help, then the parent must have been secretly defective. If an obvious defect cannot be discovered, an unconscious one can be postulated. If the "unconscious" defect is not demonstrable, then the society can be condemned en masse as hypocritical. With all those rationalizations available, you can see how well insulated against objective criticism this theory remains.

The following are two case histories that illustrate again how other rationalizations keep this theory from being discredited:

After the death of a young adult who had committed suicide while under the influence of drugs, I spoke with his father. This man was a law-enforcement officer. As part of his service to the community, he had given lectures on the evils of permissiveness.

One might suspect that the death of his son would have forced a reassessment of his views. However, this was not the case. Rather, the father told me that he had raised his son properly (i.e., nonpermissively), but that he had "let up" on him too soon. The father recalled that when the son first began wearing his hair too long and dressing "freakishly," the father had not protested vigorously enough. The father believed that he had failed his son and "lost" him that one summer when he had not forced the son to trim his hair and to dress differently.

Here is another example of a similar situation that came to my attention. Note, again, how the traditional theory escapes with its reputation intact in spite of its obvious failure:

A six-year-old boy who was attending private school had been acting very mischievously in class. Following a conference between the parents and the principal, the conclusion was reached that the child had been spoiled and that what he needed was more discipline. The principal asked that he and the teacher be given permission to use various forms of punishment at their own discretion, with the promise that their firmness would "straighten the child out" for the parents. Note in the principal's offer the implication that the parents themselves were either weak-willed or incompetent.

Parental permission was given. Subsequently the child was punished in all possible ways known to the school authorities, from loss of privileges to severe beatings with a paddle. After one month of this the child had regressed to a completely infantile level of functioning. His speech regressed, he was incontinent day and night, and almost wholly unresponsive to adult authority.

It took a year of kindness, patience, and understanding on the part of the parents, with the most sparing use of punishment, to return this severely regressed youngster to his appropriate age level of functioning.

It is to be hoped that after an experience of this sort, the authorities who recommended the "no nonsense" approach would go through a period of prolonged reappraisal of their pet beliefs. This was certainly a situation in which some learning should have occurred. Unfortunately, however, no new learning took place. The school authorities expelled the child. But they did not apologize to the parents for having been wrong. Instead, they told the parents that the child had been spoiled so badly that even the school had been unable to straighten him out. Undoubtedly the school authorities, in good conscience, will use this case as a "horrible example" to illustrate to other parents how dangerous it is to spoil a child.

It is time now for people to stop trying to place the blame for delinquency on either the parents, the child, or society as a whole. These modern attempts to find a source of evil somewhere inside the child, the parents, or society represent nothing more than a sophisticated, twentieth-century form of demonology, in which the public and some professionals are playing the role of high priests in assigning the guilt.

Although it will be difficult to do so, we must desist from our self-righteous intellectual, yet basically superstitious, attempts to find fault with the parents' intelligence or character or morals when children become delinquent. We must come to recognize that the average middle-class parent in this country is neither mentally, morally, nor psychologically defective. We should all graciously, generously, and compassionately accept the idea that the majority of those parents whose children turn away from parental values or toward the use of dangerous drugs are just as intelligent, informed, sincere, conscientious, moral, and responsible as we ourselves. If we could grant them these virtues instead of attempting to assign blame, we could focus our attention on the real "enemy": the theory and approach to child-rearing prevalent in this country which forces parents to interact with their children in ways that inevitably accentuate angry rather than loving feelings and thereby produce youthful delinquency. Moreover, we could more readily comprehend the apparent paradox that has been a source of perplexity for centuries: why it is that the most conscientious parents would be so highly prone to producing rebellious, delinquent children.

In the Introduction to this book I stated: There is no necessity for your child to become remote from you, to turn away from your most respected values, or to turn to the use of dangerous drugs—if you have the courage to act toward him in a manner consistent with those compassionate, humanitarian principles which you have learned from your own Judeo-Christian religious training.

Why is it that I recommend something as commonplace and unsophisticated as the principles of a religious tradition to the post-Freudian, twentieth-century parent? Because upon careful analysis when all the irrelevant elements are removed, the essence of the problem of drug abuse and other forms of delinquency are the feelings of love or lack of love that exist between people.

Therefore, whoever has spoken most authoritatively on the subject of love between people has also spoken most authoritatively on the subject of delinquency. In my opinion, no one has ever spoken with greater clarity or authority on this subject than have certain of the Old Testament prophets, the scholarly rabbis, and Jesus.

In various discussions in this book I have attempted to persuade the reader that delinquency is a "disease" which is produced by mismanaged feelings. I have said that the child turns toward drugs and delinquency as the relative strength of his feelings of anger gradually comes to outweigh the feelings of love he holds toward his parents.

If parents understood how positive or negative feelings were created in children, they would know also how delinquency was created. If parents could learn how to produce loving feelings and to avoid producing anger, they would have it within their power to eradicate delinquency. The most excellent guide available for parents in this endeavor is that body of ethical principles given us centuries ago by the Biblical authorities described immediately above. These principles comprise the most complete statement possible on the subject of creating love and reducing anger.

The following is a list of the basic principles which I urge parents to follow at all times in dealing with their children:

1. The Golden Rule—Behave toward others primarily as you would like them to behave toward you.

2. Maintain unswerving faith in the basic goodness of the individual no matter what his current deficiencies in behavior might suggest.

3. Be ready to forgive without limit no matter how often the individual fails to live up to a particular standard of conduct.

4. Repay anger and irrationality with kindness (turn the other cheek, walk the extra mile).

5. Be generous.

The usefulness of these principles derives from the fact that each of them does something constructive about the child's feelings toward the parents. While stated originally as "moral" principles, each of them is in reality a powerful and practical psychological "tool" that can be utilized by the parent to produce loving feelings in the child and to prevent the buildup of anger.

You will recall that I explained in Chapter 1 that it was not sufficient for the parent merely to love the child "inwardly" but that the love had to be demonstrated overtly through specific actions which revealed the love. The value of the principles I am describing here is that each one tells the parent precisely how he is to act toward the child in order to demonstrate his love to the child. This, in turn, produces those loving feelings in the child which immunizes him against delinquency. These principles given us by our greatest thinkers make up in a sense for what nature did not provide us "instinctively"—the connection between the inner feelings of love and its outward manifestation.

These principles have been thoroughly tested by time. The difficulty with them has never been that they have failed to work, but that people have been too fearful to use them. An act of faith and courage is necessary before an individual dares to depend upon them, faith that the power of love is greater than the power of fear for improving the behavior of errant individuals.

4

WHY THE BEST INTENTIONS WEAKEN CONSCIENCE

Let us examine now one possible example of an everyday situation that might confront the average parent. Following the illustration, I will discuss the weakness of the traditional approach and then the rationale that makes the Golden Rule the "treatment of choice" for dealing with such situations.

One morning a few minutes before the child is due to leave for school she suddenly discovers that her gym shoes are missing. Gradually as the deadline for departing on time for school approaches, the child becomes more alarmed, more emotional, and more disorganized. The mother-daughter dialogue might sound something like this:

PARENT: (*Angrily*) Why didn't you put them away properly last night? Why don't you ever put things away like you're supposed to?

CHILD: I did put them away.

PARENT: Well, if you weren't such a scatterbrain, you'd remember where you put them.

CHILD: Mother, please help me find them. I'll get four demerits.

PARENT: I have more important things to do. Do you want your father to be late for work?

CHILD: Oh, Mother! You probably put them away in the wrong place yourself.

PARENT: You selfish, lazy brat! Don't you dare accuse me of putting your shoes in the wrong place. I'm the one around here who always cleans up your stinking messes or you'd never find anything. Now you just go to school right now and take your demerits. And just because you accused me, you can stay in your room all day when you come home from school.

This exchange, in itself quite disturbing to both participants, is nevertheless only a prelude to a more serious, long-lasting disruption of the parent-child relationship. If you examine the dialogue, you will find that the child had committed at least five legally definable, socially indefensible, and punishable "sins": (1) She had been careless (at some time the previous evening she had misplaced her gym shoes). (2) She had been disobedient (she had ignored countless parental reminders to care for her own possessions in a neat and orderly manner). (3) She had been selfish (she had upset other family members with her behavior that morning and created the possibility that her father might have been late to work and she had demanded more than her fair share of her mother's time). But most reprehensible of all, she had (4) attempted to escape blame for her own carelessness by (5) falsely accusing an innocent, hard-working person, her mother.

In the face of all these demonstrable "sins," the conventional parental reaction normally would be to respond with (1) justifiable anger, (2) massive expressions of disapproval, (3) the providing of accurate information as to who really was at fault, and (4) threats and enforcement of various forms of punishment.

Later, in the car on the way to school, the mother might have shown her anger by glaring at the child and either refusing to speak to her or "spitting" words at her through clenched teeth. Then, at dinnertime, the entire situation would be recapitulated with the father doing the lecturing, scolding, and punishing a second time to supplement the impact of the mother's actions of the morning. Although remaining very upset by the entire affair, the parents would derive comfort from their belief that they had done their duty toward the child, that they were "putting a stop to such nonsense once and for all."

The parents' hopes and expectations, of course, were that their expressions of disapproval, their realistic discussions of who was right and who was wrong, and their administration of a moderate punishment would serve as a reminder to the daughter that she had to behave far better than she was in the habit of doing.

Unfortunately, however, the average, normal child will not respond in this manner to expressions of parental disapproval and punishment. As I described in Chapter 2, because the child is irrational he will expend a major portion of his mental energy in denying his own responsibility for wrongdoing and concentrate instead on the imagined "meanness" of his parents. It is virtually impossible for a child to accept guilt no matter how wrong he is in reality.

If we could have observed the child's emotional responses at different points as the conflict over the gym shoes developed, we probably would have observed the following:

She became angry with her mother when the mother told her that she (the child) had not put the gym shoes away properly the night before.

She became angry with her mother when the mother called her selfish and lazy.

Finally, she became angry with her mother for telling her to accept demerits at school and for punishing her after school.

Note that even though the entire disturbance from beginning to end, including the eventual receipt of punishment, was brought on and sustained by the child's own narcissism and irrationality, the end result is a very strong feeling of anger toward the mother.

As a reflection of this anger and of the child's irrational capacity for evading guilt, her thought processes while at school that day were very likely to proceed along these lines:

I just hate her, telling me I'm selfish and lazy. She's always bugging me. And she never has any time for me. It's always Daddy first, or Sister first, never me. No wonder I don't listen to her. Who wants to live in a house with that creep? Put this away. Put that away. She's so phony. Who's she trying to impress? She likes that stupid house more than she likes me. I guess she just can't stand for kids to be happy or have any fun.

In the example given of the child's "real" thoughts while at school, you will observe that there is no evidence of acceptance of personal responsibility. There is no evidence of remorse or guilt. Rather than manifesting guilt over her own actions, the child is experiencing intense anger toward her mother. Thus, what should have become a conflict between the "good" and the "bad" within the child (an intrapsychic conflict) became instead a conflict between the child and her mother (an interpersonal conflict).

The parental comments and actions, first in the numerous demonstrations of disapproval and finally in punishment, gave the child sufficient excuse to focus on angry feelings toward the parent instead of guilty feelings for a personal failure to act correctly. The end result of the parent's actions, no matter how well intentioned, was to block the development of the child's conscience (i.e., the idea that the child herself had a personal failing that required improvement). Instead, the child experienced resentment toward the mother and the values that the mother was attempting to teach.

It was as if the child had awarded to the mother that portion of her own mind we call conscience and since she was angry at her mother, she was also angry at "conscience." The parent's actions provided the child with an excuse which the irrational mind of the child could use for evading personal responsibility and growth. The net effect was not a strengthening but a weakening of conscience which pushed the child closer to that pattern of relatively conscience-free behavior which we call delinquency. This is the reason that conventional child-rearing techniques which depend so heavily on the use of intellectual explanations of right and wrong, expressions of disapproval and punishment, are usually ineffective or worse, even though to common sense they appear correct.

Perhaps the reader is now thinking along these lines: Whatever anger the child might have felt toward her parents is completely unjustified and therefore irrelevant. According to any reasonable, rational, or logical standard of judgment the child herself was completely responsible for everything that went wrong, including the fact that she was eventually punished. She asked for it, she earned it, and she got it. The mother did nothing more than her duty demanded and was completely blameless. For the child to feel anything other than remorse is to permit herself an unjustified indulgence in self-pity. If she did not feel genuine remorse, the punishment was all the more necessary in order to remind her and make her feel that way in the future. If she had to feel sorry for herself, at least the punishment would give her something to really feel sorry about.

Now if the child were a rational-thinking creature, the preceding argument would be completely appropriate and useful. The logic is unassailable. Child-raising would then be a relatively simple, straightforward, and uncomplicated matter. Unfortunately, however, nature has not provided the child with a sufficient degree of reason at an early enough age to respond appropriately to a logical system that makes such beautiful sense to an adult. The child can respond only within the limits set by its own biological nature at any particular point in its development. The parent cannot "make" a child respond more rationally by yelling at him or punishing him any more than he could make a color-blind person see all colors, using the same technique.

Obviously, it would be a far more desirable situation if children were capable of responding more rationally. It would be far better if they listened to the wise counsel of adults, if they did not get angry with parents who were merely doing their duty, if children benefited from being punished and felt genuine remorse for their transgressions, if they didn't come to resent people who loved and were trying most of all to help them. This would make life so much easier for both parents and children.

However, the profound desirability of this situation does not make it a reality. Children are irrational. They get angry at parents for the wrong reasons. They feel persecuted for the wrong reasons. These reactions cannot be ignored merely because they are unpleasant or undesirable. Neither can they be talked out of the child with intellectual arguments, no matter how cogent. Nor can they be "beaten" out of the child. This wholly undesirable factor, childhood irrationality, can only be "loved" out of his personality. Any technique of child-rearing that does not take into account this factor of irrationality, that utilizes techniques of child-rearing dependent for their effectiveness on a rational functioning organism, is doomed to failure.

I am going to describe now how a mother might have handled the challenge of the misplaced gym shoes if she had used the Golden Rule as her primary guiding principle. The thought processes of the mother, described below, may appear elaborate or time-consuming. However, in actual practice they occur almost instantaneously and do not require the constant interruption of ongoing activities.

As soon as the child called out, "Mother, I can't find my gym shoes," the mother should have begun thinking to herself, Have I ever been in a situation very similar to the one my daughter is facing right now?

Very quickly the mother could have recalled an instance such as the following: She was about to leave for the wedding reception of a friend and could not locate her purse. The mother must then ask herself: How did I want to be treated by the people around me when I needed help? What could they have done either to make me feel good or to upset me further?

How did she want her husband to treat her at that time? Did she want him to lecture and scold her? Did she want to be told that he had more important things to do? Did she want him to tell her that she had always been "scatterbrained"? Or did she want him to be helpful and sympathetic? Obviously, she would prefer that her husband say to her: "Honey, I'm sorry. Can I help you look for it?" This is the kind of treatment that would make her feel good inside and loving toward the person extending the kindness to her; therefore, this is the kind of treatment she should extend to the daughter to elicit the same feelings in her.

If the mother had been able to put herself "in her daughter's shoes," she would have been able to respond unerringly with the most humane, psychologically sound and constructive response to her daughter's predicament. And this would have been accomplished without the need for the intercession of any intermediary, whether professional mental health worker, newspaper columnist, or relative.

In response to my advice in this matter many sincere and reasonable parents have made comments such as the following: "That's all very fine for you to suggest. But you are not a mother in the kitchen trying to make lunch for everybody. What should a mother do who wanted to follow the Golden Rule but was really too busy to help find the missing shoes?"

The solution to this dilemma is not so difficult as one might imagine. Remember the goal of the parent's effort is to influence the child's feelings favorably. This is not synonymous with saying that the parent must always be able to solve the specific problem with which the child is confronted in order for him to feel kindly toward the parent. Whether or not you are able to help in a practical way, there will always be some way for you to behave which would make the child aware that you wanted to help, were trying to help, or were very sorry that you couldn't help. If you are able to convey any of these attitudes, you can bring out feelings of warmth in the child even though you can do nothing tangible to solve the reality-based problem.

Reflect for a moment: Doesn't it often occur that adults are forced to deal with problems for which there are no ready solutions available? There are chronic illnesses. There are the deaths of loved ones. These are situations in which our friends and relatives can be of no practical help. Still we may be profoundly moved at the genuine sympathy offered and the deep sorrow experienced by another person over our misfortune.

Therefore if the mother in my illustrative case was really too busy to help her daughter search for the missing shoes, she might at least have said: "Honey, I'm very sorry; I can't help you now. Please keep looking a little while longer." The mother's response here does little or nothing to solve the problem of the missing shoes. However, it does accomplish something far more important. It enhances the child's feelings of love for her and at the same time makes it very difficult for the child to direct her irrational anger against her mother and away from herself. Even though the child remains frustrated, the mother-child relationship is enhanced because the mother focuses her major effort on influencing the child's feelings.

In order to appreciate fully the value of this approach to child-rearing, remember that encounters such as the incident over the misplaced gym shoes will take place between child and parent numerous times, everyday, while the child is growing up. Their impact cumulatively is great even though any simple conflict by itself may appear insignificant. It is unfortunate that such minor daily occurrences should be related to disruption of family life, delinquency, and drug abuse. Nevertheless, in middle-class American homes where parental irresponsibility and the use of excessively harsh punishment is rare, it is the accumulation of angry feelings during these repeated minor parent-child conflicts that causes serious behavior problems. The strategy behind the daily utilization of the Golden Rule is that by concentrating on influencing the child's feelings favorably, it prevents the buildup of accumulated anger over these numerous, minor, daily conflicts, which might otherwise summate so as to produce teen-age delinquency.

Of course if children were logical-thinking creatures, this painstaking attention to their feelings would be unnecessary. The child, in my example, would have put her shoes away properly, as instructed, to begin with. Unfortunately, however, the irrational nature of the child makes this impossible. Adults wishing that it were so, becoming angry that it is not so, or even insisting that it was so in 1890, will not make it so. Childhood irrationality is a reality and careful attention to the child's feelings offers the best hope for dealing with it constructively.

The following are two other alternatives or compromise solutions which the mother might have offered, still applying the Golden Rule, in her efforts to deal benignly with her daughter's dilemma:

1. "Sweetheart, don't worry about it. If you don't find them soon, I'll write you a note asking the teacher to excuse you from gym today so you won't get any demerits."

2. "Honey, I'm sorry I can't help you look right now. I must make your father's lunch. But as soon as he's gone, I'll look for them and bring them to you at school."

Undoubtedly it is difficult to act toward children in the manner I have described here, since a strong element of self-sacrifice is always involved. However, since you do love the child, it is important that you make these sacrifices so that the child receive your love in a form he can recognize unmistakably and appreciate. The child always will be measuring your love by your actions rather than by your intent.

Try to imagine how the child might have felt toward her mother on the day the mother had delivered the gym shoes to her at school. What better opportunity could have been presented the parent for demonstrating her love to the child than the "crisis" over the misplaced shoes? What better opportunity could one imagine for producing loving feelings in the child toward the parent? And how could a child who felt such deep feelings of appreciation to the mother then rationalize to herself when alone at some crucial decision-making time, "I am not guilty because she was mean first."

The mother who decided to deliver the gym shoes was making a genuine sacrifice. This kind of sacrifice, of course, cannot be made routinely, but even if made very infrequently, it would have a powerful impact on the child's feelings. Remember, as I indicated in Chapter 1, it is not sufficient that love be experienced inwardly as a self-contained sensation. In order to have impact on another person, love must be manifested in overt actions.

It is an essential aspect of human nature that we come to know whether or not we are loved largely in terms of what is given us freely by another at some sacrifice to himself. Christians judge whether or not God loves them, in part, according to the criterion that he so dearly "loved the world that he gave his only Son." Also, Christians take as evidence that Jesus loves them the fact that he gave his life for their sins. Jesus tested the "love" of a rich man by telling him to return home and give away all his riches before becoming a disciple. The man never returned. Do we then infer that he loved Jesus? And it is written that even God applied this test of love when he commanded Abraham to give (i.e., sacrifice) his beloved son. Abraham was willing, so God knew that he loved him and rescinded his order.

In this same way, also, our children will judge and decide whether or not we love them largely on the basis of what we are able to give to them generously, freely. They will discover our love mostly through discerning our efforts at self-sacrifice. One day this may mean that you should do something apparently as absurd as driving all the way to school so that your daughter might have her gym shoes and not receive four demerits.

I must agree with any adult who would say: Logically, this is ridiculous. But, I reiterate to the logical thinker, it's not logic that restrains children from using dangerous drugs. For centuries, "the elders" have been explaining things logically to young people with very little success. It's time for adults to accept a difficult and disagreeable reality, that we must learn to deal effectively with children's feelings rather than solely with their intellects if we are to guard them against unwise, dangerous, or immoral actions.

5

HOW THE BURDEN
OF LOVE REDEEMS

Anyone with experience in life knows how appreciative a person feels upon receiving help from someone. This feeling is even greater if the help has not been earned, in any way, previously, but is offered solely because of the generosity of the giver. Recognizing this characteristic of human nature, the reader will observe that the child in our illustration (see Chapter 4) would have to feel warmly and kindly toward parents who responded to her in ways suggested by the Golden Rule. Note that in the example given, the original problem may not have been solvable in any practical way. There were certain things the parents may have found impossible to do. But these are secondary. The really important issue is what had been done to the child's feelings, and to the parent-child relationship as a result of the problem initiated by the child.

At any time, of course, the parents could have dealt with the problem by expressing disapproval, punishment, etc. But this, as I have already indicated, only makes the child angry and detracts from the child's feelings of love toward the parents. On the other hand, if the parents had been able to speak kindly or lovingly to the child, offering whatever help they could, they would have (1) enhanced the child's feeling of love toward them, (2) prevented the buildup of irrational anger, and (3) made it more difficult for the child to evade responsibility for her own actions.

The incredible beauty and value of the Golden Rule principle of our Judeo-Christian heritage is this: It enables a parent to deal with a potentially conflictual problem created by a child in such a way as to reduce conflict and increase the feelings of love existing between the family members.

You could observe that in the discussion thus far, the child presented the parents with several opportunities either to provoke anger or to enhance feelings of appreciation and love in the child. But up to this point, I have not yet mentioned the greatest challenge and the greatest opportunity presented to the parents in the entire incident of the misplaced shoes. I should like to discuss this issue now.

The most significant testing of the parent occurred when the child accused the mother of having misplaced the gym shoes. At that point the parent was confronted with perhaps the most difficult philosophical, theological, and ethical question with which mankind has ever had to deal: the question of how to respond to the sinner in order to redeem him. The reader need not believe in a traditional concept of "sin" in order to deal with the following discussion. I use the word "sinner" here primarily to stress to parents that in dealing with their own children on occasions such as described here, they are dealing with an age-old problem of mankind. I want parents to realize that in attempting to cope with and change the behavior of their children, they are dealing with a difficult problem that has perplexed some of our greatest thinkers for centuries.

In order to help the parent decide how to act at these crucial choice points, I ask that he select from among mankind's great teachers and to decide wisely just who it is he will choose to follow. Whichever technique the parent believes would bring about change, improvement, or redemption in mankind in general as "sinners" is precisely the one that would also work most effectively to change or improve his children. Adult sinners, after all, are nothing more than grown-up children who have not developed sufficient self-control to restrain their childish, irrational, hostile, destructive, and hedonistic impulses. If the parent is

Jewish or Christian, he already knows, or should know, what approach to the "sinner" is most likely to be effective in bringing about a constructive change in the errant individual. Certainly, Jesus was telling us something very important on this very issue when he forgave, rather than condemned, Mary and saved her from the crowd who wished to stone her to death. He was trying to show us something of the power of accepting, of loving, of forgiving, of withholding condemnation and punishment of the wrongdoer in order to raise his behavior to a more desirable ethical level.

Now, what does all this have to do with the child who misplaced her shoes? When that child, in anger, accused her mother of having misplaced the shoes, she had committed an obvious, verifiable, and indefensible wrong against her mother. Not only was she attempting to avoid the consequences of her own misbehavior but she was maligning an innocent, hardworking person, her mother. The parent at that point is confronted with this age-old dilemma: How do you respond to the "sinner"? How do you treat her to make sure that she sins no more? If you follow the traditional view, you lecture, you point out who is really guilty, you scold, perhaps you scream, and if that doesn't get the sinner to change her ways, you inflict pain upon her, sufficient pain to make her stop doing whatever it is she is doing.

On the other hand, if you have any faith in your own Judeo-Christian heritage, in the sayings of the venerable rabbis, or in the teachings of Jesus, you dare to gamble on the power of love and withhold expressions of disapproval and punishment. You appeal to the Golden Rule. You ask yourself and answer honestly: Was I ever in the same position my child is in now? Have I ever done a complete wrong and been discovered at it? How did I wish to be treated when I was the wrongdoer?

I recall discussing an issue like this at one time with a young woman whose life pattern had changed rather dramatically from one of delinquency and sexual promiscuity to one of stability and responsible service toward others. The turning point in her life came, she said, one night after she had gone to a "wild" party. Her parents, who were members of a fundamentalist religious group, routinely had forbidden her to go to parties and particularly to drink alcoholic beverages. One night she had lied to them and on the pretext of going with some "nice boys" to a Bible study class had gone instead to a party where she became heavily intoxicated. When she returned home, she had just enough strength to admit herself to the house, where she fell on the living room floor and vomited. The parents discovered her lying on the floor, stupefied, in her own vomitus. Contrary to what they had ever done before, the parents, without comment, lifted her gently, washed her off with cool water, undressed her, and put her to bed. They gave no lecture the following morning. While their faces and manner indicated concern, they did not show bitterness or disapproval. During that morning, the young woman reported, she began to believe, for the first time she could remember, that her parents loved her.

Surely in everyone's life similar incidents, perhaps not quite so dramatic, must have occurred. Parents must be willing to search their own past experiences for such events and then ask themselves honestly how they would have wished to be treated by those people whom they themselves had failed. When the parent was the "sinner," did she want a firm application of the law, "You made your mistake and now you'll pay for it," or did she want total forgiveness without condemnation? Did she want to be cast away from them forever? Was it necessary that those she had failed should repay in kind before she felt genuine remorse and tried to atone?

Very often during counseling sessions with parents who are members of certain traditional Christian denominations, I have asked: "How do you wish to be treated by God when you are face to face with him? What is it you will want from him? Will you want every sin and transgression to be held against you eternally, or do you wish to be included under the umbrella of mercy? 'Father, forgive them; for they know not what they do.' If this is your prayer for what you yourself would want, if this is what you would appreciate to the depths of your own soul, then this is what you should attempt to give the child to whom you are 'Father.' The child will appreciate it and be as thankful to you as you would be to a merciful God. Why should you give the child anything less than you yourself will ask for?"

How should the mother have acted after being accused, unfairly, by the daughter of misplacing the shoes? How can she best redeem the sinner? Obviously, with kindness and forgiveness in spite of and in the face of the daughter's wrongful accusation. The kindness might have been demonstrated simply by the mother's not replying to the daughter's comment. This is a way of saying silently, "I heard your comment, but I do not condemn you for it." Of course, the mother's facial expression during the silence must not itself reveal condemnation. The mother must be mobilized and committed as a whole person to accepting the child's remark in order for this approach to be useful. If the mother in my example was capable of an additional degree of "giving," she might have responded to the child's accusation by saying calmly: "Dear, I know you're very upset right now. I'm going to help you look for the shoes in just a few minutes."

Human nature is so constructed that one feels a profound sense of appreciation toward another human being who has offered kindness. It creates a feeling of obligation to return something of value to the individual from whom one has received something freely given. This is the meaning and the message in Jesus' method of dealing with those who failed. You will recall that Peter failed (i.e., denied) Jesus three times. Did Jesus reprimand him? Did Jesus punish him? Did Jesus cast him out of the circle forever? The answer is: Of course, he did not. And what does the Bible record as having happened subsequently? Peter was strengthened. He grew so great in stature that he became a major force in developing and sustaining the new church.

If the mother in our example had been able to respond to her daughter along the lines suggested by the Old and the New Testament, the child could not possibly have devoted her mental energies, while at school, to ruminating over angry feelings toward the mother. Nor could the child have used angry feelings to hide from herself her own culpability. She would not have been able to console herself against guilt by portraying herself as the innocent victim of parental persecution. Instead of providing the child's irrational mind with "ammunition" with which the child could justify herself, the mother would have provided love. This unbalanced equation—that is, the child having committed a wrong and being repaid not in kind, but with love—creates the conditions in which healthy guilt may grow. The child is forced to come face to face with her own failings rather than with the imagined failings of the mother.

Try to imagine what a child so generously treated might contribute to a group discussion in which teen-agers were gathered to complain about mistreatment at the hands of their parents. True, she could lie about how she was being treated. But this would very likely serve to make her feel even more guilty for hurting (i.e., failing) people who had already been exceedingly kind to her. If the reader believes that the child would just go on endlessly hurting the people who were kind to her, I would again ask you to review your own experiences. How many times were you able to hurt someone who was repeatedly kind and loving to you? If you did fail such a person, several times, how guilty did you feel about it, and how hard did you struggle to stop hurting him?

Parents must train themselves to recognize that those occasions on which the sinner "sins," that is, those occasions on which the child reveals his irrational nature, present magnificent opportunities for demonstrating love and thereby enhancing the growth of the child's conscience.

It takes no special merit on the part of a parent to verbalize to a child the words, "I love you." And it requires no special merit for a parent to love a child when the child is behaving properly and doing exactly as the parent wishes. The really awesome challenge to the parent comes when the child periodically reveals his "natural" self to the parent (i.e., narcissistic, negativistic, primitive, unreasonable, and implacable). Here again, the parent finds himself in a position with his child for which a Biblical quotation is appropriate: "If you love those who love you, what credit is that to you? . . . For even sinners do the same. . . . But love your enemies."

The use of the word "enemies," of course, does not apply to our children. But you can see how appropriate this quotation would be if we substituted "rational" and "irrational" for "those who love you" and for "enemies." Then the Biblical injunction paraphrased would read as follows: What good is it if a parent loves his child when he is rational and hates him when he is irrational? Even a nonloving person can do that. One must love the child even when he is irrational.

The possibility for the growth of that inner system of behavioral controls we refer to as conscience occurs whenever an individual who has committed some wrongful act is in the presence of someone with courage enough to respond to him with love (forgiveness) rather than with anger (infliction of pain).

Theologians and psychologists agree, and recorded history demonstrates vividly, that man is born with the capacity or potential for committing immoral, unethical, or inhumane actions. Centuries ago, these tendencies were attributed to the devil's taking possession of an individual. Today psychologists refer to the person's "id" impulses. These are the same concept. Only the label given the phenomenon has been changed. But this inherent potential for acting immorally is only part of man's makeup. He is also endowed with the potential for developing a conscience.

Man's behavior is a resultant of the interaction between these two forces within his personality. If the conscience develops strongly enough, the primitive forces will be kept in check and the individual will act morally, responsibly, etc. If the conscience is weakened or if it is circumvented, then the more primitive forces (i.e., narcissism, cruelty, hedonism) will emerge victorious.

The capacity for feeling guilt, present to some degree in all people, makes it difficult to commit a specific wrongful act. However, if the individual can redefine (i.e., rationalize) the act so that it appears right, he can perform it without experiencing the pain of guilt. Thus, during the Inquisition, torture and murder were practiced in good conscience as being in the service of God. For centuries slavery was defended as a God-given institution. When Hitler and his followers decided that Jews were evil and had no right to live, they felt free to exterminate them without guilt. Similarly, when the Russians invaded Czechoslovakia and eliminated political freedom there, they defined their actions as a "liberation." In our own country many people who would ordinarily be repulsed by the idea of murder, nevertheless accepted the assassination of Martin Luther King because they believed he deserved it.

The idea expressed in the statement, "I'm not guilty, because he is guilty also," is the classic mechanism for evading conscience used by wrongdoers in all ages. It was the brilliant insight of the Old Testament writers and of Jesus to recognize that if you could deny the second part of that statement "because he is guilty also," you could force the wrongdoer into a confrontation with his own "badness." This confrontation would create at least the possibility that growth of conscience could emerge. Only by withholding punishment and offering love can you deny the child the opportunity he will be looking for to evade his own guilt by thinking irrationally, I'm not guilty, because she yelled at me and punished me. If the parent is able to sympathize, accept, and forgive over and over, the burden of love placed on the child becomes too great to resist and the child's irrational defenses against conscience formation are overwhelmed.

There will remain many parents who will disagree with the position I am taking here. They will say such things as: "You just can't let a kid get away with these things forever. . . . If I don't teach her the right way to speak to an adult, she'll never learn. . . . The kindest thing I can do for her is give her the hard knocks she has to get while she's young, so it will be easier on her later."

I would insist, however, that by repaying "sin" with loving-kindness, you are making possible the growth of conscience, whereas disapproval and punishment destroy its roots. By repaying wrongdoing with loving-kindness and forgiveness, you are giving no more than you would want given to you. And you are aligning yourself with the Old Testament prophets and with Jesus. If you believe in the Judeo-Christian tradition of God's compassion for man and God's insistence on man's expression of compassion toward man, you must see that it is the power of love rather than the power of fear of pain which moves people toward goodness or Godliness.

As a parent you must function somewhat as a sculptor. You will be presented with a quantity of material that has certain potentials. Whether or not the beauty of these potentials is revealed in time depends to a great extent on what you do with it. The raw materials of the child are its various behaviors. You are responsible for shaping this behavior from its original, primitive, unacceptable form into a very sophisticated constructive expression of human nature. You must make a very basic choice while the child is still very young as to whether you will place your faith in the power of fear and pain or in the power of love. If you have the courage to look inside yourself and to trust those leaders toward whom you have turned traditionally for guidance, then you already know the correct path.

In order to utilize the Golden Rule effectively in everyday practice the parent should have a very definite idea as to what it means. The Rule is that you are to treat the child as you yourself would like to be treated if you were in the same position or in a very similar position.

Note that the Rule contains the phrase, "like to be treated." It does not say "as he deserves to be treated." This is a crucial distinction. Frequently, we do not wish to be treated as we deserve. We are not always good. If you respond to the child by giving him what he deserves, you may reveal to him nothing of your humaneness and compassion. You are merely showing him that you have some latent talent for being a judge.

Insofar as is humanly possible, you should imagine yourself

to be in the child's position and treat him only as you would like to be treated. Don't ask yourself whether or not your response might spoil the child. Don't ask yourself whether or not your child will believe that he is "getting away with something." Don't decide how to respond on the basis of the latest article in the daily newspaper or the weekly magazine. Don't do what you think your friends, neighbors, or relatives would think proper.

On any given day different authorities will present different opinions on the same subject. Also, expert opinions will change in time. There are fads in child-rearing theories just as in other areas of life. This is very confusing to parents. It tends to make them feel very timid and inadequate when dealing with their own children.

One of the major reasons that parents encounter difficulty as they attempt to utilize the Golden Rule philosophy is that they tend to undergo a very benign amnesia concerning their own thought processes and actions as children. Adults tend to believe that they were just as rational-thinking at age two and a half as they are, say, at age forty. Often, then, it is impossible for a parent to recall with any degree of accuracy how he would have liked to be treated in a certain situation when he was a child. In such cases the parent should try to imagine himself currently in a similar relationship to another adult, and try to ascertain his own feelings and desires. For example, if a child asked his mother for extra money after spending his allowance, the mother should try to recall how she felt when she had to ask her husband for more money after exceeding her household budget.

Often, when the child-parent situation is transposed to husband-wife, the results are informative. On one occasion, for example, a father asked for advice concerning the proper bedtime hour for his eleven-year-old son. He described how his son had asked permission to remain awake later and that he (the father) had replied that he would "run a survey in the neighborhood" to find out the average bedtime of the other children. His son would then be permitted to stay awake the average time.

In order to put the father in the child's position, I drew this parallel: Supposing one evening you approached your wife and said to her very pleasantly: "Honey, I don't think we're having sexual relations as often as I would like. Let's try to do it more often," and his wife replied cordially: "Well, dear, I think I'll check with the neighbors and find out about what the average frequency is per couple. Then you and I can have it about the average."

It is possible to make decisions that appear fair and reasonable, as was the case with the father attempting to set a sensible bedtime limit for his son, and yet do injury to the feelings of the people involved. It is possible to be wholly right, intellectually, and yet to be wholly wrong on the more important issue of dealing with the individual's feelings. Why is this so important? Because feelings cause behavior!

The father's mistake was not that he failed to act responsibly toward his son, not that he failed to use good judgment, and not that he wanted to deprive his son of extra enjoyment in life. His sole mistake was that his response to the child had not taken into account the child's feelings. If he could have imagined himself in the same position, vis-à-vis his wife, he could have reacted correctly, instantaneously.

The consistent application of the Golden Rule will be advantageous for the following reasons:

1. It will provide the parent with a consistent means for understanding the child's feelings at every moment from birth through maturity.

2. It will enable the parent to function independently of mental health professionals and other advice givers and also independently of transient fads in child-rearing practices. It appears very unlikely that the Old Testament prophets and Jesus will be superseded as moral leaders in the foreseeable future.

3. It provides the parent with a dependable, easy-to-understand guide for creating loving feelings in the child at all times.

4. It provides a simple, effective technique, not only for neu-

tralizing the impact of the child's irrational thought processes but for utilizing such irrationality to produce loving feelings toward the parents.

5. Finally, the approach to child-rearing embodied in the use of the Golden Rule philosophy provides the conscientious parent with the security of knowing he is utilizing a proven, dependable, and humane approach to raising his children, a philosophy that permits him to know he is fulfilling his responsibilities both to his children and to the broader society.

6
THE IMPORTANCE
OF MOTIVATION

If you study closely the problem of influencing a child's behavior, you will discover that five basic means are available:

1. The parent may speak to the child. He may teach, explain, lecture, or instruct. He may inform the child, verbally, with the use of logic or reason, about what the child should know concerning life. He may point out the possible consequences of the child's behavior: for example, that fire burns, that children who run into the street may get run over, that hard work leads to success, that marijuana is illegal.

2. The parent may punish various forms of behavior verbally or nonverbally. For example, when a child misbehaves, the parent may give him a "dirty look," may refuse to speak to him for a period of time, or may scold or reprimand him. The parent may withhold a "privilege"; thus, a child might be forbidden to leave his home or to play with his friends. Or he might be slapped or spanked.

3. The parent may reward the child either verbally or nonverbally. The parent might smile broadly as she observed the child speaking politely to an adult. She might say, "Oh, you are such a nice boy." The child might be given a dollar for every "A" he received on his report card.

4. The parent may set a good example by eating with the proper utensils, by chewing his food with his mouth closed, by

speaking politely to others, by working hard, by obeying the law, etc.

5. Finally, the parent may motivate the child: that is, speak or act toward the child in such ways as to create in him the desire to act in the constructive manner the parent desires.

Of the five techniques listed, motivation is the most important but the least understood. In the everyday practice of child-rearing, neglect of this factor has the effect of rendering the other four techniques useless. If the parent does not understand how to act toward the child so as to motivate him to behave properly, the child will not pay any attention to the wise instruction the parent is providing; he will become more hostile and negativistic in response to the application of punishment, and he will either ignore or choose a pattern of behavior opposed to that of the parental example.

Usually, parents believe that they are motivating the child when they explain things to him calmly and rationally, when they refrain from the use of excessive or harsh punishment, when they punish him only when he deserves it, when they reward him when he has earned it, and when the parents themselves have behaved properly. Unfortunately, this is not the case. These techniques should not be defined as motivational because they have no effect whatsoever in making the child want to behave the way the parents believe he ought to behave. No approach to child-rearing that fails to deal with the feelings of the child, particularly as influenced by his irrational thought processes, may be considered accurately to be a motivational approach.

This is not to say that children raised without particular attention being given to the variable of motivation will never behave properly. Often, while under direct or indirect adult supervision, when faced with the prospect of imminent punishment, such children will behave quite well. But these four techniques alone, in the absence of motivation, contribute nothing toward helping the child develop and strengthen his inner system of behavioral controls (conscience), so that he might be better able to make responsible decisions when alone and unsupervised.

This, after all, is the crucial issue: How morally responsibly is the child able to function when he is entirely on his own in the community? All parents recognize the fact that you cannot supervise even a young child, but particularly a teen-ager or young adult, twenty-four hours a day. Sooner or later the child will be dealing with people and decisions in the "outside" world all by himself. Inevitably, as occurs in all lives, temptation will present itself to him. It may occur while he is in the schoolyard or on the playground, on a street corner or in a car, even inside his own home. At that crucial point in his life, the child's decision for good or for ill will depend almost entirely on the motivation that has been built into him previously. If he has been motivated properly, he will accept the logic of the lifelong parental teachings and resist temptation. On the other hand, if he has not been properly motivated, he will still be aware of the parental instructions, of the possibility of punishment, and of the parental example, but he will ignore them all.

The difficult part of child-rearing consists in the parents' learning how to deal with the child in such a way as to motivate him to act in a desirable manner. Centuries of neglect of this factor have led to an oversimplification of the role and definition of a good parent. Telling the child what is right or wrong or socially acceptable or unacceptable requires no extraordinary skill or talent. Nor does figuring out different ways to punish the child for misbehavior. The real challenge of good parenthood occurs in the area in which the parent learns to deal constructively with those delicate and largely irrational feelings which the child will experience while growing up. This is the crucible of motivation.

Often, parents are surprised to find that even point number three, rewarding good behavior, is not considered a benign motivational influence. "Surely," they say, "rewarding a child is preferable to punishing him." This is true. However, my experience indicates that reward does not act as the parents would hope. Children (being irrational) tend to equate the use of reward as not very different from that of punishment in that both represent coercive efforts at controlling their behavior. It is this factor of control which they come to resent. Some children have compared such a relationship with their parents to an adult's relationship with a bank. We may be thankful that a particular bank loaned us money which we, of course, repay as our part of the bargain. But such a relationship does not inspire loyalty. We don't come to love the bank. It's logically sound and fair, but children want more than this from their parents. If parents wish to inspire their children, to imbue them with an inner urge toward right living, they must be more than logical and fair with their children.

A brief period spent listening to or reading information being disseminated by the mass media should convince the reader that most of what purports to be a psychologically sophisticated approach to child-rearing consists of nothing more than elaborations of techniques 1 and 2, described previously, i.e., speaking to the child, teaching, lecturing, explaining, or instructing, pointing out to the child the painful consequences of various forms of misbehavior, and punishing him in various ways. The underlying assumption in these approaches is always the same —that the young person's awareness of either the severity or extent of the pain he is likely to experience as a consequence of his actions will act as a deterrent.

The following are two examples of materials appearing routinely in the mass media which illustrate this approach. Both, of course, are sincere, competent, and logically sound.

The first is an article that appeared in the "Dear Abby" column of the *Los Angeles Times*, August 4, 1970. In this article Abby presents an exhaustive list of all that a young person stands to lose if convicted of marijuana use:

Dear Sixteen: He stands to lose: The right to vote. The right to own a gun. The right to run for public office. The right to become a licensed doctor, dentist, C.P.A., attorney, architect, realtor, private detective, pharmacist, school teacher, barber, or any of a number of career job opportunities. He may be forbidden the opportunity to work for the city, state, or federal government. He cannot be admitted to West Point, Annapolis, or the Air Force Academy. He would be permitted to enlist in the military service, but would not have a choice of service.

Not to mention the loss of approval of family, friends, potential friends, and society at large.

This is a high price to pay for "trying grass" . . . or even agreeing to "hold it for a friend," which is often the case.

Think about it.

The second example is a column by William F. Buckley, Jr., in the *Los Angeles Times*, July 29, 1970. In it he presents a beautifully written, moving letter from a deeply concerned father. Notice how well the father, obviously an articulate and intelligent man, mobilizes his arguments to the sons:

Dear Sons: M.N., after your spring vacation, suggested to me that you were both smoking pot. Your headmaster, John, let fall a cryptic remark whose innuendo I chose not to accept. Your final report, Jim, excellent as it is, does mention a lessening in your community participation over the past several months. The main complaint from your headmaster about you, John, is that you have this past year "retired" from the school and school activities and withdrawn into yourself. These attitudes of withdrawal are precisely those outward manifestations mentioned in the Toronto medical report I left with you before saying goodbye in New York. If you have read that report carefully, you will realize that the effects of pot or hash are deleterious mentally and psychologically, as well as being cumulative. . . .

Returning to hash and pot, let me remind you of the following:

1—The laws, rightly or wrongly, are stringent, and they

are being energetically prosecuted. If you are caught in possession of these drugs, or smoking them, you are liable to severe fines and prison sentences.

2—Medical evidence—such as the Toronto report—mounts against these drugs, indicating severe psychological and intellectual consequences.

3—Your Uncle Herman is a national figure in the musical world; your Uncle David is running for national political office. Your responsibility is not only and exclusively to yourselves.

4—To the extent that you are mature young adults and responsible for yourselves, you ought to have the moral courage, really minimal, to reject any temptation toward this sort of dangerous and unlawful nonsense.

Since you began growing into adulthood, I have prohibited you very few things, relying on your judgment, your prudence, and your sense of right and wrong. If you write me back to tell me that what I quoted above is a bunch of horsefeathers, I'll be thankful and, of course, believe you. If you write to say that you once experimented with pot but have quit it, I'll believe you, I'll be thankful, I'll be grateful that you have stopped; but I will be amazed that you have permitted "peer pressure" to so overweigh your judgment. . . .

Should either of you have once indulged in pot or acid, or in pot more than once, you are commanded by me to stop, but I want to be taken into your confidence. . . .

Something perhaps drove or drives you to drugs, something we may be able to handle together in mutual trust and affection. The distinction in gravity between acid and pot is wide; but even in the case of the less-grave pot nonetheless unlawful; nonetheless injurious—I am unable to come to your help unless you extend to me the confidence I extend to you.

Lovingly . . .

Any rational-thinking person would have to recognize immediately that everything the father (and Abby) was saying was absolutely true. Yet these obvious truths do not have the power to sway. What is lacking in well-intentioned efforts such as these? The answer is that they fail because they appeal solely to the logic or reasoning ability of the child but do nothing meaningful with his feelings. Since they do not alter the basic feelings that are the driving force of his overt behavior, they do not motivate him to behave differently.

Let us look again, briefly, at the case of the family we became acquainted with through the father's letter in William Buckley's column. Should we assume that this intelligent and obviously responsible man had never before warned his sons in any way either directly or indirectly about the dangers of drug abuse? Should we assume that the sons of this probably well-to-do family had never once heard their parents express concern or regret over the problem of drug abuse among young people, never had an opportunity to read a newspaper or magazine article on the subject, never once saw a program on television describing the drug scene, and never once during their entire school careers had heard even one lecture sponsored by the local authorities which attempted to discourage children from getting started on drugs? Clearly such assumptions defy credibility. Isn't it obvious, also, that the father and other adult members of this family had set good examples by being law-abiding, ambitious, and responsible citizens?

It would appear to me far more reasonable to assume that these boys, like most children in America today, had had a very considerable rational education on the dangers of drug abuse, long before they ever experimented with their first "hit." The question that must be asked is not: Why did these boys fail to receive a proper logical education? The greatest likelihood is that they did. The more relevant question that must be asked is: Why did these young men choose to ignore the family example and all that had been logically presented to them?

Parents are justifiably perplexed when after following their own common sense and socially sanctioned theory of child-rearing, the children do not turn out as desired. The solution I am proposing is that the parents in complete innocence have overlooked the most important factor of all—motivating the child to behave properly.

A proper understanding of the crucial role of the child's feelings and thereby his motivation in shaping behavior should enable the reader to examine conventional discussions on the subject of discipline or punishment with greater perspective.

Conventional approaches to the subject of punishment are often quite narrow in scope. Usually, they limit themselves to a consideration of only three questions.

1. Is punishment ever necessary?
2. Do parents have the right to administer punishment?
3. What is the most effective method of punishment that can be devised?

Typically, the discussant musters a series of arguments that lead to the first two of these questions being answered affirmatively. All attention and intellectual effort then is turned toward dealing with question number three. What is the most effective method of punishment that can be devised? The subject of the child's feelings, particularly the question of the impact of punishment on the child's feelings, is completely ignored.

Let us look briefly at how the question of discipline and punishment is handled typically when concerned parents seek advice from various authorities. Suppose, for example, that a "Desperate Mother" posed the following question to the child guidance expert of the local newspaper. "My five-year-old refuses to go to bed when I tell him to. Do I have the right to make him go or will this traumatize him?" The reply would read approximately as follows: "All children require punishment. You as a parent may not shirk your parental responsibility. Get yourself a sturdy paddle, and if the child continues to disobey, give him some 'friendly persuasion' on his bottom."

If you will recall now the three questions I posed previously, you will find that the expert answered the first two "yes" and then went on to deal with the third, suggesting his own preferred mode of punishment. As is typical in such discussions, the expert assumes that when the first two questions are answered affirmatively, all other considerations regarding child-rearing become irrelevant with the exception of determining the most powerful form of coercion that may be utilized. But the existence of a "need" for punishment and a right to punish does not automatically validate the wisdom or effectiveness of the procedure guaranteed by that right. Policemen, for example, have the right to shoot at people when, in their own judgment, it becomes necessary. But the existence of this right does not demonstrate that shooting people is the most desirable technique of law enforcement. Similarly, parents do have the right to punish. But this does not eliminate the need for independent judgment on the part of the individual, whether parent or policeman, to assess the desirable or undesirable consequences of the exercise of that right. Parents must still attempt to answer for themselves these important questions:

1. Does repeated punishment increase feelings of love or feelings of anger?

2. Does it increase happiness or create depression?

3. Does it raise or lower the child's feelings of self-respect?

4. Do the feelings created by punishment act to enhance or inhibit the child's desire to cooperate with the parent and adult society in general?

If the subject of punishment were studied in the broader context suggested by these questions, parents very likely would come to different conclusions regarding their use of disapproval and punishment than are currently popular. At present, however, a majority of parents and experts still are limiting themselves to the narrow, three-step approach I described earlier. The result is a kaleidoscopic proliferation of suggestions from an infinite variety of authorities all of whom offer the promise that their newest form of punishment will be more effective than the one proposed by some other authority. In the next chapter, I will present the reader with several examples of the kind of advice commonly offered. Note that in none of the illustrations that follow is any consideration given to the question of how the parent should interact with the child routinely, so as to help motivate him to want to become a decent, responsible human being.

7

THE PARENTAL ROLE
BEYOND PUNISHMENT

Let us look now at the kinds of advice typically given to parents on the subject of discipline and punishment.

The most gentle of the experts stress the use of verbal reminders and reprimands. They recommend that parents admonish their children with mild reproaches such as, "I was not proud of you today," or more forcefully, "I was very ashamed of you today." In general, verbal punishment is preferable to other methods. However, as I will attempt to demonstrate later in this book, once the parent is encouraged to believe that he is "licensed" to use this technique, he uses it either in excess or too crudely. Thus, when aroused, parents feel justified in making statements such as, "You are nothing but a tramp," "I detest the sight of you," or "You don't have the brains that God gave little green apples."

These same experts would also advise the use of various threats. In the book *Parents on the Run*, the following example is given:

A mother of four children had the right idea in this respect. The first day of school, each year, she lined up her brood. . . . She issued this ultimatum: "Go straight to school. Do what the teacher asks of you. You are not the only children in the class. She has no time for monkey-business on your part. If I ever hear that you have made any unnecessary trouble for your teachers, I promise I shall make twice as much trouble for you when you come home." She always kept that promise to them, too.[2]

What joy, what bliss if raising children were this simple!

A great many experts suggest the use of various forms of punishment the roots of which lie in two rather old ideas:

1. An eye for an eye, a tooth for a tooth, and

2. Let the punishment fit the crime.

The parental action called for may be relatively benign or extremely harsh.

For example, if a child fails to eat enough food, the parent is advised to deprive him of food. Or if the child tends to choose overlarge portions or to eat excessively, the parent is to force him to eat more to the point of nausea if necessary. If the child uses bad language, the mother is advised to wash out his mouth with soap or to put black pepper on his tongue. If he is caught sampling an alcoholic beverage, he should be made to drink more, to get the full impact of the burning sensation in the throat. Many authorities (usually the lady-next-door) advise that when the very young child hits or bites the parent, the parent hit or bite him back.

A great many experts today suggest the use of what I call "stratagems." These are built around a psychological core more sophisticated than simply biting the child back. What makes stratagems so intriguing to parents is that they appear to be methods of getting children to do what the parents want them to do, without the necessity for issuing overt threats or for actually administering a specific form of punishment. The following is one fairly typical example described in *Parents on the Run*:[2]

On a rainy day Captive Mother was busy with household tasks, but Junior kept interrupting her, whining and asking her to play with him. Captive Mother suggested several different ways in which the child might have entertained himself, but he was not interested. Independent Mother, on the other hand, devised the following plan to help Junior function on his own:

Knowing that the child disliked doing household chores, she suggested that he take a rag and help her dust the furniture. The child then immediately lost interest in being with his mother. He went off by himself and played happily all afternoon. Mother was then free to do what was really important, her housework, without having to listen to her child's constant whining. She explained to the child: "I'm sure I don't know what you should do to amuse yourself. It really isn't my problem. My problem is this work I have to do." The mother refused to act as "an unpaid entertainer for the afternoon."

The trouble with such stratagems is that only the parent is deceived. The child will become aware of the rejection and humiliation to which he has been subject in spite of the attempt at subterfuge. His emotional state and feelings toward the parent will be correspondingly impaired.

A large group of experts, attempting to coax parents away from the old-fashioned notion that the most effective form of punishment is physical abuse, are now recommending withdrawal of privileges as the best all-around form of punishment to use. The major premise underlying this approach is that if you deprive the child of something he enjoys, he will learn to behave properly. In order to be maximally effective, the child must be deprived of something that he values highly. Thus, these authorities recommend that parents take the bicycle away from the child who loves it; take television privileges away from the child who most enjoys watching it; withdraw telephone privileges from the child who is at the stage where the telephone is of crucial importance to him. (Why is it that pleasures are always defined as privileges?)

These experts may disagree among themselves as to the deterrent value of different forms of deprivation, the optimum time period during which deprivation should be imposed, and also whether or not to permit the child to experience other pleasures while being deprived of the major one.

Many authorities agree that since children are so gregarious, the most potent form of deprivation is social isolation. They recommend confining the child to his own home as the best possible form of punishment. These authorities differ among themselves on the length of time a deprivation must be imposed in order for it to fulfill its function as a truly corrective emotional experience. There are some (a minority) who would say that one full day would be enough. Others would insist that no less than one full week is required before any form of deprivation is truly felt by the child.

The unfair feature of this approach is that the probabilities are always overwhelmingly against the child. Once the isolation period has been extended—to, say, one week—there is very slight chance that any normal youngster can avoid being "bad" even once. What parent is perfect for an entire week? Yet, how tempting for the parent during the period of the child's confinement to keep extending the period of punishment, over even the smallest deviation from the parent's wishes. For example, if the parent observed the child frowning, or if the child slammed a door too hard in his frustration, or if the child hit his baby sister, the parent might be very much inclined to say: "Oh, you think you're unhappy now. Well, I'll really give you something to be unhappy about. We'll just make that two weeks that you're grounded now. And any more show of that nasty temper of yours and I'll make it four!"

On several occasions families have consulted me while one of their children was still in the middle of an extended period of social isolation. The child might have been in, say, the sixty-third day of a ninety-day "sentence." Upon questioning, neither the parents nor the child could remember the child's original infraction or even the second or third which had led to the ever-increasing penalty being assessed. All the parents and the child knew was that they were thoroughly disgusted with one another and were looking for some way to extricate themselves from the exhausting and frustrating game they were playing of convict and jailer.

The genuinely old-fashioned hardliners, of course, have not yet left the scene. There remain among us a significant number of experts in various professions who still believe that the only proven, dependable technique of child-rearing is corporal punishment. Here is a portion of an article that appeared in the *Los Angeles Times*, September 2, 1970:

> Municipal Judge _____ Tuesday, told two girls arrested for curfew violations they should receive old-fashioned spankings. [The Judge] told the mothers of the two eighteen-year-old girls they should "get a strap and beat the hell out of them." He told one mother, "Let her know she's a woman, not a bum. We've got enough tramps and bums around here."
>
> The Judge advised the other girl's mother to "knock some sense into her. It's the only way to make anything out of her."

The judge did not make clear, at least in the article as reported in the *Times*, how treating a young woman in such an unladylike manner as to "beat the hell out of her" was going to impress upon her the fact that she was a woman and not a bum.

Among advocates of the use of physical violence there still exist areas of disagreement as to how much pain the child should be made to experience, what kind of instrument should be used, and what portion of the anatomy should be struck. Some recommend the use of the hand on the buttocks. Others advise a stick or paddle. Some authorities recommend an open-handed slap in the face accompanied by some remark such as, "Remember, I'm still your mother." A slap in the face not only hurts the parent's hand less than does a conventional spanking but it adds the additional deterrent power of humiliation, especially if administered publicly as the child gets older.

The most sophisticated experts of all even advise parents how they are to feel while punishing the child. According to these authorities, a blow administered while the parent is in the heat of genuine anger will have greater impact and do less emotional damage to the child than a similar blow delivered when the parent is calm and rational.

This "Chamber of Horrors," this obsessive search for the most exquisite, nonlethal form of pain that can be administered legally to a child is presented to the public, daily, as if it were the whole or major subject matter of contemporary child psychology.

In my discussion in Chapter 6, I outlined the five major techniques available to parents for influencing their children's behavior. They were: (1) speaking to the child (lecturing, reprimanding, threatening, etc.); (2) administering verbal and nonverbal forms of punishment; (3) granting rewards for good behavior; (4) setting a good example; and (5) motivating the child.

The reader should now be able to recognize that public attention has been focused almost exclusively on the first two of these five devices, both of which depend for their success on a process in which the child is notably deficient—the logical functioning of his mind. Little, if any, consideration is given either to the very important issue of motivating the child or to the significant component of irrationality in the child's manner of responding to the parents' efforts.

But, being reassured constantly that they have the right and the duty to discipline and to punish, responsible parents come to view their major contribution to child-rearing as that of administering discipline and punishment. What happens then is that as parents persist in exercising their right to eliminate the imperfection, the child becomes the recipient of an endless stream of parental disapproval and punishment during all the years he is growing up.

This destructive process begins at that moment when the parents decide that it is time to start the child's preparation for adulthood. Probably the first parental decisions made on this matter concern whether or not the child will be placed on a "fixed" versus a "demand" feeding schedule and whether the child will be picked up and held or ignored when he cries. Traditional advice, of course, would suggest that the mother who places her infant on a "demand" feeding schedule and who picks up the crying infant has taken the first steps down the treacherous road of permissiveness.

But as all parents know, the challenges presented by the child and the need for parental decisions as to how to cope with the child's behavior have barely begun at that point. In ten thousand other ways the child will continue to reveal his imperfection and his need for guidance. (He will urinate and defecate at the wrong times and in the wrong places, he will be disobedient, he will talk back, he will do his chores poorly or not at all, he will have temper tantrums, he will lie, he will come home late for dinner, etc.)

On all such occasions the parent will experience no difficulty in determining that the child's actions are wrong. And having been taught to assess his own response to the child's actions exclusively in terms of whether or not he has the right to punish, the parent will not hesitate to disapprove of and to punish all the child's misbehavior. The parent will reason that since it is his duty to eliminate wrongdoing, he is justified in assessing any degree of disapproval or punishment on the occasion of any childish misdeed. But seduced by his own sense of rightness, the parent will remain chronically unaware of the narrowness of his conception of the parental role and of its undesirable consequences.

The result is that the child is pressured, threatened, intimidated, coerced, and punished repeatedly every day of his life as part of the continuing effort to make him obedient to parental dictates. Unable to conceptualize the relationship in any other terms, the parent continues to act toward the child in ways that are inadvertently quite sadistic.

This long-term, sincerely motivated but sadistic approach ultimately produces the excessive feelings of anger and distrust of the parents that injure both the parent-child relationship and the child's personality itself. And this destructive process is set in motion by the uncritical acceptance of two simple propositions that are logically defensible as far as they go: (1) Growing children will require that some limits be set on their behavior, and

(2) Parents do have the right to establish such limits, with the use of punishment if they so desire.

The narrow-minded, inflexible acceptance of these two propositions serves to keep parental attention focused, perpetually, on the fruitless search for the perfect form of punishment available, with an unawareness on the part of the parents that the indiscriminate use of punishment itself is the primary enemy of their children's mental and emotional health.

After the child has lived many years with an oppressive, conflictual kind of relationship with his parents, his feelings of anger finally become ungovernable and are revealed in some distortion in his behavior: in his relationship with his family and, often, in the indiscriminate use of dangerous drugs.

At that very late point in the child's development, when in many cases it is already too late, the parents ask plaintively: What did we do wrong? All we ever did was to try to teach him the difference between right and wrong. We clothed him. We fed him. We loved him. We always wanted the best for him. Why doesn't he like us? Why won't he listen to us now? Why is our child the one who is on drugs?

This entire book, of course, represents an attempt to answer this question. But very briefly, I would say to such parents: Children have feelings that cannot be ignored. It is not enough that parents exercise their rights to establish standards of conduct and to enforce conformity to such standards through the use of persistent disapproval, criticism, threats of punishment, and the administration of punishment. Such an approach untempered by an awareness and consideration of the child's feelings, no matter how defensible intellectually, will serve primarily to create excessive feelings of anger in the child. This anger will disrupt both the intimate family relationship and the personality functioning of the growing child. The outward form of this disruption will be some form of delinquent or "sick" behavior.

Delinquency, including the indiscriminate use of dangerous drugs among young people, is an outgrowth of the normal process of child-rearing. It occurs in those instances in which the parents have acted sincerely, logically, and responsibly but have failed to temper their actions with sufficient understanding and compassion for the child as a sensitive and fallible human being.

The study and the application of different techniques of punishment have always made up the essence of the traditional approach to child-rearing. As an alternative, I am recommending that parents begin to study just as intensively what the child-rearing process itself does to the child's feelings and, therefore, to his personality development.

Parents now should try to understand that the most important series of events taking place within the growing child is the continuing struggle for dominance between feelings of love and feelings of anger, and that the primary function of the parents in raising psychologically healthy children is to affect favorably the outcome of this inner conflict.

Recognition of this principle will affect parental functioning in two very important ways: (1) It will expand the parental role far beyond the narrow limits within which it has been conceived traditionally, and (2) It will place a greater burden of responsibility on each parent for using individual judgment and discrimination.

First, let us examine the expansion of the parental role. It follows logically from what I have just proposed that virtually all parental actions toward the child are important because most of the conceivable parental actions hold the potential either for enhancing love or for creating anger in the child. This means that a parent is being a parent at all times and not only on those occasions in which he is teaching, lecturing, reprimanding, punishing, etc. The demand and the opportunity for functioning as a good parent occurs whenever the parent and the child are in contact or in communication with each other.

Many fathers (and some working mothers) believe that they are fulfilling their parental responsibilities adequately when they return home from work in the evening and institute a cross-examination: Was Johnny a good boy today? Did he clean up his room? Did Sally practice her piano today? Did she prepare the dinner? Did she vacuum the rug? Did Bobby do his homework today?

This traditional conception of the parental role and responsibility is far too limited. The teaching or "lawgiving" function of the parent is only one segment of the parental role, and, as I have indicated previously, the one that operates primarily to produce anger and to reduce love. It is not sufficient that parents who conceive of their role so narrowly point out that the "lawgiving" function is necessary (which it is) or that their demands are socially desirable (which they are). If the parents' actions produce excessive anger and the anger produces delinquency, all the logic in the world will not salvage the child or alleviate the parents' distress.

When the parent recognizes that the major contribution he has to make to his child's emotional well-being consists in enhancing love and in dissipating anger, the importance of all other occasions of parent-child contact not related to the teaching-punishment aspect of the relationship can be seen and appreciated. Even the least-significant-appearing fragment of parent-child interaction may be recognized as containing the potential for making some contribution, positive or negative, to the existing balance of love and anger within the child.

For example, the parent would have to consider the impact on the child's feelings of such apparently insignificant things as the tone of voice she uses when awakening the child in the morning or when "tucking him in" at night and the expression on her face when she greets the child upon her return home from work in the evening. The parent would have to pay attention to her typical manner of speaking to the child or of responding to his needs or requests. For example, when the child asked for a rather expensive toy, would the parent respond by saying, "Gee, honey, I'm sorry but I just can't afford to get that for you now, but maybe I can surprise you by Christmas," or would she say: "Do you think I'm made of money? Do you think I was put here on earth just to be able to buy you things?"

Whether or not the child gets the toy he wants, the parental attitude revealed in part in the words used to deny the request may serve either to enhance love or to increase anger. Parents should recognize that an important part of their responsibility consists in presenting those words and attitudes to the child which can help him to keep his own anger within manageable proportions. The parental duty is not fulfilled merely because the parents have denied the child's request and given logical justification for their actions. The parental duty is completed only when, in addition, the parents have dealt with the child's feelings in the most constructive manner possible in a given situation. (More will be said on this point in Chapter 13.)

Often parents become both confused and irritated because, in their own minds at least, they are convinced that they have not defined the parental role too narrowly, and yet they have experienced disappointing results with their children in later years. Such parents insist, for example, that they did more than merely teach the child right from wrong. In addition, they tried to make him happy by spending time with him in activities such as scouting and by taking him to places children enjoy. In spite of this, however, the parents discover that their child became emotionally disturbed in some way, or even delinquent.

The common error in parental thinking on this matter consists in the parents' believing that their engaging in child-centered activities is in itself enough to demonstrate their love and to create warm feelings in the child. Undoubtedly engaging in such activities with children helps. However, there is always a great deal of seemingly minor and peripheral interaction occurring that the parent tends to overlook.

Consider a planned trip to Disneyland, for example. To what extent are parents usually aware of the potential impact on the child's feelings of parental actions (1) prior to the trip, (2) while at the amusement park, and (3) in the car on the way home. How many times during the week preceding the trip was the child warned that if he didn't "straighten up," he wasn't going to get to Disneyland. How much "mileage" did the par-

ents get out of the anticipated trip to ensure that the child per-
formed better than he did usually: for example, in doing his
chores. On the morning of the trip to the park, how many dirty
looks did the child receive for such actions as getting out of bed
too slowly, failing to clean up his room, failing to wash or to
comb his hair thoroughly, failing to feed the dog, fighting with a
sibling over who was going to sit next to the window in the car.
Later, at the park, how much scolding did the child receive for
running ahead too fast or lagging too far behind, for asking for
too much money for "junk," or wanting to go on "just one more
ride," for whining and complaining, or for being thirsty and
having to go to the bathroom too many times? And still later, in
the car, on the way home when everyone was tired and irritable,
how many reprimands, threats of punishment ("I'll never take
you to Disneyland again as long as I live!"), and actual punish-
ments did the child receive for losing his balloon, being ungrateful, fighting with his siblings, etc.?

Many years after this day at Disneyland very likely there will
exist a difference in perception as to what kind of day it had
been and what it had added to or subtracted from the feelings of
closeness between the parent and the child. The father will remember with a feeling of pride and satisfaction how much he
had tried to be a good father. He had taken the child to the
amusement park on a very hot day, spent time with his child,
and been generous. The father now hopes that the child's feelings about that day will be shaped by these three aspects of the
father's actions.

Unfortunately, however, the child will remember, and his
feeling will be affected by more than the father intended or
would want. The child will have imprinted somewhere inside his
nervous system everything that passed between the parents and
himself that day and the days preceding. Everything will have
had some impact—the reprimands, the lectures, the threats, and
the administration of punishment.

Years later, if the son should come to feel that his father had
been "mean" to him, the father would not know why. The father would find it astonishing that the child could forget such

happy experiences as the wonderful trip to Disneyland and all the money that had been spent on him. The father would conclude erroneously that children have poor memories or that they are inherently ungrateful. In reality, the difference between the parents' and the child's perception occurs not because the child recalls less than had happened but because he recalls more of what happened.

Often the difference in perception and reaction to past events is labeled with the wholly misleading phrase, "A breakdown in communication." The common acceptance of this phrase leads parents to believe that their continuing difficulties with the child reflect primarily their own inability to discover that particular combination of words which would make the child see that the parents' actions and points of view and intentions always had been correct. The term implies that the misunderstanding between generations is related to an inability to find certain words on which both child and parent could agree; and that the disputants could be brought closer together through a careful selection and use of words, particularly if the child was willing to listen.

The mutual misunderstanding, however, is not a matter of semantics. By the time the child has become chronically angry with his parents, he has been the recipient of a myriad of parental actions that have made him so. These feelings have a reality of their own. They took place, they were recorded, and they exist now somewhere inside the child's nervous system.

The child's feelings will be determined solely by his history of actual experiences with the parents. These may not be the feelings which the parents intended for the child to develop. However, the child's feelings are linked to his actual experiences with the parents (i.e., with the parents' behavior) and not with the parents' intent. Once these feelings have come into existence, words alone are insufficient to change them. Only other actions on the part of the parents can alter the original feelings (anger) that developed and replace them with new feelings (love).

Remember, it is not simply taking a child to an amusement

park, to the beach, or to engage in scouting activities that asserts a benign effect on the parent-child relationship. This effect is determined, in addition, by the quality of parent-child interaction at all times preceding, during, and following such activities. It is very dangerous for parents to overlook any longer the need for dealing sensitively with their children's feelings during the numerous minor occasions of parent-child contact that take place hundreds of times every day.

By stressing repeatedly the importance of considering the child's feelings, I hope to make parents more aware of those insignificant-appearing areas of interaction which usually are given insufficient attention during the child-rearing process. This should help parents avoid making those numerous, minor mistakes that create frustrating differences in perception between the parents and their children as to what "really" happened while the child was growing up.

8

THE LOVE BANK

Does this need to remain aware of the child's feelings imply that parents must live in constant dread of making the child angry? Am I suggesting that a child will become delinquent and turn to the use of drugs if a parent makes him angry once, twice, thrice, or even a dozen times each week? The answer to these questions is "No! Of course not."

A growing child will experience and can endure comfortably a great deal of frustration and anger. All of us do during our lifetimes. This is a normal part of the human growth experience. Any child will develop and carry with him a great deal of anger which will not damage or distort his personality development to any significant degree. A completely anger-free human being simply does not exist. Nor is there any particular reason to strive for such a theoretically "pure" state.

However, what parents must come to understand is that the child's capacity to tolerate anger is not infinite. There are different degrees, or intensities, of anger that people may experience. And there does exist some particular degree of anger which, once exceeded, is likely to result in some distortion of the child's personality.

Where the child's emotional health is concerned, the primary responsibility of the parent is to make certain that the child's level of anger does not approach or exceed this point.

There is no single parental action that is likely to generate a sufficient degree of anger to make the child turn toward delinquency. It is highly unlikely, also, that any limited series of parental actions would produce anger too intense for a child to live with and remain healthy. It is not necessary for parents to live in constant dread of "traumatizing" their children through one inadvertent misstep or even through a fairly extensive series of minor "mistakes." As I have stated repeatedly, there is no such thing as a perfect parent. All parents, either through inadvertence or because reality demands it, will act in such ways as to make their children angry. But fortunately, nature has not demanded that parents be perfect in order to raise psychologically healthy children. A great deal of tolerance for error is built into the system.

Nevertheless, parents must realize that a continuous pattern of anger-producing parent-child interaction, pursued unswervingly because it is based on incorrect assumptions about the nature of the child's thought processes, will inevitably produce a degree of anger sufficient to cause delinquency.

One way to conceptualize this situation would be to imagine the child as a kind of "love bank" in which the parents might make deposits or withdrawals. Each day the parent is provided with numerous opportunities to make either deposits (love) or withdrawals (anger). As long as there is a surplus of love in the account, no serious problem is likely to occur. However, if the account becomes seriously depleted or overdrawn, anger will prevail and delinquency will occur. In terms of this analogy, the major function of the parent is to use his entire person in his everyday relationship with the child in such a way as to ensure that there is always a substantial surplus of love in the account.

Several of the usually puzzling aspects of child-rearing will become more understandable if the parent will keep the above analogy in mind.

Often, parents find that repeated use of punishment either is having no beneficial effect on their child or seems to make him behave worse than ever. Yet they can recall that at some previous time in the child's life, their use of punishment had had the desired effect in suppressing misbehavior. The parents cannot understand why punishment no longer "works."

The explanation for this phenomenon is that at some point in the child's development his love account became overdrawn. All that remained (or at least what remained in greatest abundance) was anger. The cushion of love was gone. Once that point was reached, punishment no longer asserted a restrictive force on misbehavior. Instead, punishment acted to intensify the existing anger and therefore generated more misbehavior rather than less. Yet on some previous occasion when a surplus of love still existed, the same degree of punishment administered by the same parent in the same situation would have exerted the restrictive effect the parent desired.

Similarly, parents often observe that their neighbors use certain forms of punishment and seem to achieve an excellent degree of control over their children. Yet when these parents use the same technique as their neighbors, they find that punishment fails to work as well for them. Why, they ask, can the neighbors get better results than we can using precisely the same approach?

The explanation for this apparent paradox is the same as the one given just previously: the neighbors have not (as yet) overdrawn their love account. Therefore, punishment still works for them. It retains the power to assert a controlling effect on their children's misbehavior. In many ways unobserved by the puzzled parents, their neighbors must be making more deposits than withdrawals. If the neighbors also began making excessive withdrawals, their children, too, would begin to react by becoming more unmanageable when subjected to the repeated use of disapproval and punishment. This is a law of nature. No set of parents can escape its effect. The belief that one can do so is merely an exercise in unproductive wishful thinking.

It would be exceedingly desirable if mental health workers could define for parents in some tangible way the amount of love that is needed as a cushion, or the amount of anger that is intolerable. Unfortunately, however, no such objective measures exist. All that parents can do, given the present state of knowledge in the psychological science, is: (1) To follow the basic principle that in any given situation they should act in such a way as to enhance love and/or to reduce anger whenever reasonably possible. (Note that in living up to this rule, the parent will be required, at all times, to exercise considerable independent judgment as to what is reasonably possible. The need for exercising such independent judgment cannot be avoided.) (2) To become aware of the early warning symptoms that the child might reveal in his behavior which would indicate that his anger was beginning to reach, or had already surpassed, the point at which love could still exercise some moderating influence.

What this means in the everyday practice of raising a child is that from the time the child is born, the parent should be willing to review, constantly, his own behavior toward the child and to estimate what impact this behavior is having on the child's feelings. Honest application of the Golden Rule should indicate with a high degree of accuracy the impact of the parental behavior on the child. The parent must then strive diligently to do whatever is necessary to create those positive, loving feelings he wants the child to have. There is no need for this constant review to lead the parent into an obsessional frenzy of self-doubt and guilt because the essential principles of sound child-rearing are so very simple. All that the Golden Rule calls for is that the parent be willing to temper his intellectually and morally motivated actions toward the child with elementary human warmth, kindness, and forgiveness.

Young children will reveal a wide range of behavior which gives clear warning that their anger has reached unmanageable proportions. Here is a list of commonly occurring symptoms. While reading this list, the parent should keep in mind that it is not meant to be an exhaustive list, but merely suggestive.

Neither should the early appearance of any symptom on the list be interpreted as suggesting that it might occur earlier or be more serious than some other symptom appearing later in the list. These matters are quite unpredictable at present:

1. Prolonged difficulty falling asleep.
2. Persistent nightmares.
3. Bedwetting after a long period of having been "dry."
4. Sleepwalking (in my experience a rare occurrence).
5. Irrational or incapacitating fears (phobias). These fears might attach themselves to almost any object or situation. Commonly they occur in connection with going to school. The child becomes too fearful to leave home and may become physically ill to the point of vomiting as the school hour approaches. Sometimes the fear of leaving home is camouflaged with other irrational fears. For example, the child might refuse to leave home, "because I might meet a dog on the way to school," or "because there might be a fire in the house and mother would be killed while I was in school." Sometimes the phobia centers around the occurrence of a more improbable catastrophe (i.e., "While I was at school, the sink might fall out and Mommy would be drowned").
6. Repeated acts of disobedience. For example, the child might become surly and argumentative in response to virtually all parental requests and orders. Getting the child to carry out the trash might become a major ordeal for the parent, requiring constant nagging and reprimanding before it was done. Then the child would do it reluctantly and poorly.
7. Repeated talking back, sarcasm, mimicking, and, on occasion, threatening and even hitting the parent, using "foul language" to the parent.
8. Repeatedly indulging in acts of minor mischief at home, at school, and in the neighborhood. At home, for example, the child might scribble on the wallpaper or "poke" holes through a screen door with a pencil. The child might throw dirt clods onto a neighbor's front porch or into the swimming pool. At school he might scribble dirty words on the lavatory walls or stuff the toilets with old rags.
9. Misbehaving repeatedly at school. Being the class "clown," talking out of turn, refusing to stay in his seat, failing to finish his assignments, fighting a great deal with other chil-

dren, talking back to the teacher, earning very low grades after several years of having earned substantially better grades. Beginning to associate primarily with other children who are not well accepted by the majority group but who spend much of their time violating established school rules.

10. Becoming even more slovenly in caring for his room and in matters of personal hygiene than is expected with normal, forgetful, careless, disorganized children.

11. Excessive teasing and fighting with siblings. The importance of this symptom is usually difficult to assess because sibling rivalry is so common an occurrence. If it occurred by itself, in the absence of other questionable behavior, I would suggest that parents not be too concerned about it.

12. Associating primarily with children much younger than himself and avoiding competitive situations with children his own age.

13. Becoming depressed and withdrawn. Making statements such as: "Nobody likes me"; "I hate myself"; "I wish I was just dead"; and "I wish you had never borned (sic) me."

14. Periodic running away from home or threatening to run away.

15. Frequent temper tantrums not necessarily accompanied by crying spells.

16. Frequent episodes of petty theft at home, at school, or in the neighborhood.

17. The occurrence of psychosomatic symptoms, such as recurring headaches. The significance of physical complaints must be evaluated first by a physician. If, in the physician's opinion, there is no organic basis for the symptom, an emotional basis for it (i.e., anger) should be considered.

18. Excessive preoccupation with sex in some form (i.e., excessive masturbation).

The reader may be surprised to find that several of the warning signs included in this list refer to feelings of anxiety in various forms (i.e., phobias) and depression as well as the emotion of anger. Yet in previous discussions in this book, I have referred almost exclusively to anger. The reason for deferring mention of these two additional emotions was for the sake of clarity in presenting my ideas to the reader. In everyday experience these three emotions—anger, anxiety, and depression —will almost always occur together. The angry child most often is anxious and depressed as well. The symptom picture will vary, so that in individual cases one or the other of these three emotions will be more apparent. However, regardless of which one appears to predominate, all three should be considered as present and contributing significantly to the child's problem behavior. The key to understanding the buildup or decline of all three emotions lies primarily in understanding what the parents have been doing to cause variations in the balance between love and anger.

Anger, anxiety, and depression tend to occur together in the child because they have a common etiology, conflict with the parents. During the child's formative years, his feelings of self-respect and self-confidence are determined primarily by the quality of his relationship with his parents. If the child comes to believe that his parents "see" him as a worthwhile person, he will perceive himself also as a person worthy of self-respect and of the respect of others. He will define himself as a person of value if his parents' words and actions toward him have helped to define him as a person of value. In a similar manner, the child will feel more self-confident as he attempts to deal with the challenges of everyday life when he feels that, if he should need his parents' help, he has the close support of these two strong allies.

But what happens to the child's feelings of self-respect and self-confidence if parental actions have been of such nature as to generate a great deal of anger? These feelings are severely injured. The injury to the child's self-respect produces depression. The injury to his self-confidence produces anxiety.

These three "problem" emotions—anger, anxiety, and depression—co-vary because the same parental actions that produce anger also, simultaneously, (1) give the child the feeling that he is unworthy of being loved and (2) create a feeling in the child of being separated from the parent.

Whenever a parent expresses disapproval, lectures, scolds, reprimands, criticizes, or punishes the child, the child suffers some loss of self-respect. The greater the amount of disapproval, etc., shown by the parent, the greater the loss in the child's feelings of self-respect. The more profound the loss in self-respect, the more profound the feelings of depression to which the child will be subject.

Whenever a parent expresses disapproval, lectures, scolds, reprimands, criticizes, or punishes the child, the child experiences some degree of separation from the parent. The greater the feeling of separation, the greater the loss in the child's feelings of self-confidence in his own ability to cope successfully with the challenges of everyday life.

To the extent that a child feels unworthy of being loved, he will feel depressed. Depressed people, whether adults or children, carry within themselves an excess of self-hatred rather than self-love. If this self-hatred reaches sufficient proportions, the adult (and less often the child) may even attempt suicide. Often an individual who attempts suicide does so while contemplating or immediately following an attempt to kill someone else. These cases demonstrate in extreme form the close relationship between anger and depression existing within the same individual. A person who becomes extremely angry with others is also depressed and equally angry with himself.

Whatever parents do to a child in order to make him become very angry leads him to feel that they do not want to help him or even that they enjoy hurting him. Many rebellious youngsters believe that their parents are sadists who get their "kicks" from punishing children. When children begin to interpret the parents' motives in this way, they tend to separate themselves from the parents. They come to see the parents primarily as persecutors or oppressors to be avoided rather than as friends or allies on whom they can count for help.

To the extent that this separation occurs, the child will be cut off from the primary source of support which he will need in order to feel that he is competent enough to struggle success-fully with the demands of the "real" world. Being separated (emotionally) from his parents, believing himself to be cut off from their support, the angry child will "see" himself as smaller, weaker, more alone, and more helpless than other children his own age who possess physical and intellectual capabilities no greater than his own.

To summarize briefly: The child who has developed a great deal of anger, because of long-standing conflicts with his parents, in addition to being angry is also (1) markedly lacking in self-respect or self-esteem, and (2) markedly lacking in self-confidence. Because of this, he is very vulnerable to severe feelings of anxiety as well as of depression.

Reflecting his own perception of himself as an individual who is weak, helpless, isolated, and unlovable, he is likely to antici-pate that nothing but frustration and repeated failure will result from his participation in everyday life. Anticipating failure, the child may simply become incapacitated by excessive anxiety (as is the case with some school phobias) and simply withdraw. Such withdrawal may occur at different times in the child's life. Typically, these withdrawal tendencies reveal themselves at transitional points when the child is confronted with the neces-sity for taking a clearly definable step forward in life: for exam-ple, upon beginning nursery school or kindergarten, or upon leaving elementary school for junior high or high school, or upon graduation from high school or college and facing the task of looking for a job. The most noticeable "dropouts" at these various points are the angry, anxious, depressed children.

In the majority of cases, however, the underlying feelings of low self-esteem and low self-respect are masked, and the avoid-ance of competition is reflected in a more disguised manner than through the development of excessive anxiety, phobias, and open withdrawal manifested in frank refusal to participate. Rather, it takes a form that the adult community defines as re-belliousness, negativism, nonconformity, and early delinquency.

The largest group of angry, anxious, depressed children at-tempt to cope with feelings of weakness and anticipation of failure by such means as denying any interest in pursuing worth-while goals. This is nothing more than the old "sour grapes" mechanism by which the child attempts to avoid frustration by saying, in effect, "You don't have anything I want." These children will define activities such as working for good grades or athletic prizes as "dumb" or "square." In contrast, they will define "doing your thing" or "getting stoned" as "wild," "groovy," or "out of sight," thus deliberately bringing about their own failure in order to retain control over the situation. This device helps the child to feel less vulnerable or impotent when dealing with the world which is frightening to him. The child's underlying defensive maneuver might be stated as follows: "I could have made good grades if I had ever wanted to, but I didn't." The definition of scholastic attainment as "dumb" and successful children as "square" helps to support this line of defense. On the other hand, the child can guarantee himself a great deal of success by working for undesirable goals, those which are easily attainable because few, if any, children in a given class are striving for them. For example, angry children might be the most successful in defying their teacher or other school authorities. Growing their hair too long and successfully defying the authorities' efforts to get them to cut it is exceedingly rewarding to such children. Again, it helps give them a feeling of mastery over their environment which they can achieve in no other way and which thereby helps them reduce their growing feelings of weakness. Other similar kinds of behavior which fall within this category are teasing and bullying smaller children, being the first in class to smoke cigarettes surreptitiously on the school grounds, and likewise being the first to try pills, "grass," or heterosexual activities. The feelings of loneliness, worthlessness, and unlovability are compensated for by seeking out other rebellious, nonconformist children who are busily expressing their own angry feelings in a similar manner.

During early adolescence, these rebellious children tend to come together in same-sex pairs. The parents of each member of the pair are usually convinced that their child has fallen in

with bad company. Assiduous efforts are made to prevent asso-
ciation with the "bad influence." Such efforts, of course, are futile. One child is not "making" the other bad. Rather, both have
found each other. Each satisfies important needs for the other.
Having an ally helps each feel less lonely. Having an ally makes
each feel more powerful in his efforts to cope with the "outside"
world. Having an ally gives each child reassurance that he is
fully justified in his rebellious assault against authority.

During later adolescence and young adulthood, these pairs
become enlarged into mixed-sex groups and "communes" of
various kinds which serve the same supportive function for the
individual as did his earlier single companion.

Now we have a more complete picture of the angry child at
various stages of his life: feeling unloved and unworthy of being
loved; excessively anxious and depressed; an underachiever,
avoiding competition for worthwhile social goals, but competing
actively for more easily attainable, undesirable goals; uncooperative, argumentative, negativistic, and rebellious, remote from
parents, from other adults, and from all but a few like-minded
peers; markedly lacking in feelings of self-respect and self-
confidence and anticipating nothing but frustration and failure
to result from his efforts.

It should not be considered remarkable that such an
individual, during the teen-age period or young adulthood,
should affiliate with a drug-oriented, subcultural group. Participation in such groups satisfies many of the emotionally disturbed teen-ager's needs.

1. It provides companionship as an antidote to loneliness.

2. It provides an "ingroup" of people who will promise love,
a substitute for the natural family in which love was less accessi-
ble.

3. It provides a semiorganized framework for demonstrating
various forms of hostility against the majority group.

4. It provides group-sanctioned rationalizations that justify to
the individual his own hostility, failure, and withdrawal from active participation in life.

5. Drugs themselves provide some relief from chronic feelings

of anxiety and depression. The group provides justification for the use of such drugs which, in addition to being illegal, are very likely to be injurious to the user and/or his progeny.

6. Various fake messiahs and assorted cultists offer these frightened youth an "opportunity" to find feelings of relative peace or security by accepting the messiah or cultist as their leader and abandoning their individual wills and the need for further independent effort to cope with the world.

7. The constant movement of these groups from one neighborhood to the next or from one city to the next gives the individual member the temporary feeling that he has somewhere to go, that his life is not completely formless and empty of purpose. This pointless roaming is reflected frequently in statements such as: "San Francisco is good people" (when the speaker is in Los Angeles), or, "I didn't like Santa Barbara; I got bad vibrations there." The preferred city is constantly changing. The sole criterion by which it is chosen is that it is somewhere other than where the youngster is now. The constant parties given by an endless number of "friends" (actually the most transitory of acquaintances) serve the same defensive function, providing a momentary feeling of purpose which relieves briefly some very deep feelings of depression.

If the symptoms of the child's developing anger are revealed and recognized early and proper corrective action is taken, they can be eliminated with relative certainty for the remainder of the child's lifetime. However, if no corrective action is taken by the parents or if, as commonly happens, the wrong "corrective" steps are taken, two outcomes are likely to ensue: (1) The symptoms gradually get worse and the emotionally disturbed child becomes a more seriously disturbed adult ("Poor Jenny, she was always strange, even when she was a child. . . . I remember . . ."). (2) The early warning symptoms disappear for a few years, but persist as latent tendencies which reappear in more virulent form during adolescence or young adulthood.

9

A NEW LOOK AT CONSISTENCY

What should parents do if they observe any of these warning signs persisting in their children over a period of time? They must review very carefully what their own behavior toward the child had been for several years preceding the appearance of the symptom. They must ask themselves and answer honestly, using the Golden Rule as their criterion: What have I been doing every day to make the child angry? What have I been doing that could have destroyed love? Remember again that neither the parental intent nor the inherent rightness of the parental demands will mitigate the effects on the child of the parental behavior. It is the effects of the parental behavior and not its intent or its rightness that must be analyzed.

The parents should focus their attention on the most commonly occurring areas of parent-child conflict: those which occur repeatedly and which reflect primarily the parents' efforts to raise the child correctly. The parents must acknowledge to themselves without self-deception how many times each day the child was the recipient of some form of disapproval. How many "dirty looks" did the child receive routinely? How many sarcastic, critical, or derogatory remarks did he hear? How many scoldings, reprimands, "talks," and lectures? And how much punishment did he receive for his irrational behavior, his selfishness, bad temper, carelessness, wastefulness, willfulness, bad manners, laziness, lack of concern for the rights or possessions of others, lack of appreciation, irresponsibility, poor attitude, minor mischief, lying, teasing, and showing disrespect toward his parents?

After this careful and honest assessment is made, the parents should then dedicate themselves to reducing the amount of disapproval, scolding, punishment, etc., as much as is reasonably possible. To the extent that parents are able to restrain themselves, the child's anger will be reduced. The less the anger, the less the likelihood of delinquency.

Note that in the preceding paragraph the phrase "as much as is reasonably possible" was used. A flexible criterion like this is necessary when parents accept the idea that their primary function is to deal effectively with their child's feelings. The need for exercising independent judgment becomes extremely important. Rigid, irrevocable sets of rules that would dictate a fixed response or group of responses, suitable for all parents to use on all similar occasions, simply are not available. Nor would they be useful if they were available, because they would not take into account the individual differences in values held by different sets of parents. Obviously, different parents hold different values and ascribe varying degrees of importance to various of the values held.

In one family, for example, the parents might find it intolerable if their child failed to attend church on Sundays. However, they could accept with a lesser degree of discomfort the fact that their child slammed a door when angered. In some other family, however, the parental attitudes might be the reverse. They might find an overt display of temper intolerable and yet remain relatively tranquil over the child's failure to attend church on Sundays.

Precisely which demands are to be eliminated and which forms of misbehavior are to be accepted without expression of disapproval or punishment is a matter left entirely to the discretion of the individual parents. Remember, it is not the presence or absence of any particular demand, the use of any particular form of punishment, or even the periodic use of disapproval and punishment themselves which injures the parent-child relationship. It is rather the total number, the cumulative mass of parental demands over an extended period of time, which come to be experienced as oppressive to the child. Delinquency and other disorders are likely to occur in those cases in which the parents fail to exercise restraint or moderation in their demands, but instead insist on conformity to all or to most of the virtues known to our society.

In the paragraphs immediately preceding, I have argued that when the child begins to misbehave persistently, the wisest course of parental action is to demand less, to disapprove less, and to punish less! The reader will recognize that these suggestions represent the exact opposite of those usually prescribed by proponents of the more traditional approach to child-rearing. According to traditional doctrines, when the child misbehaves, the parents are supposed to clamp down, to increase their demands, to disapprove, and to punish even more forcefully than before. This traditional recommendation is based on the assumption that the child's misbehavior reflects not anger but the fact that he has been "spoiled," that "he has had his own way for too long," or that he enjoys "taking advantage of his parents."

The reader now has a clear-cut choice as to which approach he will use with his own children: (1) the approach presented in this book, which rests on faith or trust in the basic goodness of the individual and the power of love to bring out such goodness, or (2) the traditional approach based on distrust and fear of evil in the child from which he must be purged through the use of pain.

There can be no debate with the argument that all children must learn those standards and limitations on their behavior which will enable them to function effectively in a civilized community and that parents are the societal representatives responsible for teaching and thus perpetuating these desirable values. This is a necessary and continuing part of human existence. Moreover, children can grow and thrive while learning to live within these various limits, standards, and demands. However, the child is likely to become emotionally disturbed (1) if the overall number of demands, limits, standards, etc., are excessive; (2) if these limits, demands, and standards are instituted too early in the child's life, before he is capable of responding to them successfully; and (3) if they are applied rigidly, mechanically, or painfully, untempered by sufficient compassion on the part of the parent.

The following brief summary of the experience of one family illustrates what happens typically when these principles are ignored:

A nine-year-old boy was referred for psychological treatment by his pediatrician. The child had been subject to repeated and very severe headaches. Thorough medical examination, including a complete evaluation by a neurologist, had revealed no organic basis for the persistent headaches. The headaches were relieved after a period of several months, during which time the parents accepted counseling and altered some of the demands they had been making on the child.

The parents were respected members of a very conservative Christian denomination. In attempting to raise their son properly, they had enforced not only the conventional middle-class virtues such as neatness, cleanliness, politeness, thrift, obedience, and good grooming but also values related more specifically to their own preferred version of Christian ethics.

The following is a very brief description of some of the standards to which the child had been expected to conform: During mealtimes he had to eat everything on his plate, including vegetables, which he detested, and all other "good" food chosen by Mother. He was to eat what was presented without whining or complaining. He was supposed to chew with his mouth closed, sit up straight in his chair, keep his elbows off the table, and keep both feet on the floor at all times. He was expected to refrain from giggling, laughing, and other forms of "silliness" while at the table. He was to eat slowly and chew carefully, yet not so slowly as to keep Mother or others waiting after they had finished their dinner. Following each meal he was to thank Mother for having prepared it.

Since the parents had a particular aversion to sinfulness in general and violence in particular they expected their son to observe the following code of conduct. He was not permitted to watch most programs on television, nor was he permitted to go to any movies. Even "good" movies were forbidden because they would serve to encourage moviegoing as an acceptable pastime. He was not permitted to own toys or to play games with his friends such as "cops and robbers" in any way suggestive of violence. He was instructed never to fight and, even if attacked, he was to turn the other cheek. Any display of temper was prohibited. Even speaking rudely to his friends was considered unacceptable and too closely related to violence. He was to play fair and be a good loser. He was made to attend church every Sunday and tithe 10 percent of his fifty-cent weekly allowance.

Failure to conform to any of these standards or responsibilities was followed very regularly by some form of punishment. Punishment was usually mild, but almost all known forms were used. If these parents had been more moderate in their demands, this child might well have internalized his parents' high ethical standards and survived his childhood without experiencing a severe emotional disorder. However, the parents were neither restrained nor moderate and the child became first angry and then physically ill. It was the total mass of parental demands, each one correct, each one socially desirable, each one ethically valid, which combined to produce an intolerable burden for the child. In many cases the result is (in later years) drug dependency and other forms of delinquency. In this case it was an early psychosomatic disorder.

Counseling with these parents took the form of helping them to decide which of their demands were essential to the child's physical and spiritual health and which were "nice" but not at all crucial. The parents were not asked to abandon any of their religious values. This would have been unfair to ask and impossible for them to accomplish. However, they were able to accept the idea that they could not have their own way on every issue. They had to compromise. If they were going to insist that the child attend church every Sunday, they could not insist also that he chew with his mouth closed. If they were going to insist that he stay home when his friends went to the movies, they could not insist also that he eat everything on his plate, including the detested vegetables, etc.

After several months, the child became headache-free. This occurred as he became less angry with his parents and less guilty over his normal childhood impulses. This child was "cured" because the parents were flexible and able to compromise. They retained their Christian values and they persisted in their efforts to raise the child as a responsible and ethical member of the community. But at the same time they were able to reduce markedly the number of occasions each day on which they felt the need to show disapproval, to reprimand, to criticize, and to punish. Because this compromise was effected, both the parents and the child were able to coexist under the same roof without the necessity for any one of them becoming ill.

As is usually the case, it is easier to prevent a problem from developing than to "cure" it once it has occurred. Long before any warning signs of excessive anger have revealed themselves, prudence would dictate that the parents be aware and concerned about love and anger. The responsible parent must be ready to study daily the impact of his own behavior on the child's feelings. Parents must dedicate themselves, conscientiously, to reducing their well-meaning but anger-producing actions to the smallest number per day that is reasonably possible. Keeping in mind the struggle going on between the forces of love and of anger within the child, the parents should realize that the interest of mental health demands that they reduce the list of virtuous, socially desirable demands they will make on their child to that absolute minimum which will still protect the health, well-being, and safety of the child and other members of society.

In succeeding chapters, I will present the reader with several examples of how I would recommend that parents deal with certain commonly occurring situations which traditionally would call for some form of disapproval or punishment. Before proceeding to these examples, however, I believe it would be helpful if parents became better acquainted with the concept of consistency.

Centuries of experience have shown that children tend to misbehave repeatedly in the same manner in spite of vigorous parental countermeasures. In their efforts to cope with repeated misbehavior, parents have developed confidence in the concept of consistency. A parent using this technique dedicates himself to responding in exactly the same manner on all occasions on which the child shows some particular form of misbehavior. For example, every time a child fails to eat his vegetables, he is sent to his room without dinner. The primary value of this approach is that it facilitates learning and thus helps the child to eliminate those forms of behavior which the parent finds objectionable. This approach has proven reasonably reliable. As a result, there now exists fairly widespread agreement as to its usefulness as a technique of child-rearing.

However, it is not recognized commonly that there exists not one but two different kinds of consistency. Failure to recognize this often leads to inappropriate use of the only type of consistency the parent is aware of, and the result can be extremely detrimental to the child's welfare.

The first type might be called fixed-response consistency; the second, variable-response consistency. An individual may be said to be behaving consistently under either of two conditions: (1) when he repeats the same action again and again (i.e., at seven A.M. every weekday morning Mr. Jones gets into his car and drives to his office); or (2) when an individual engages in a series of dissimilar actions all of which end at the same goal (i.e., at seven A.M. on Mondays, Wednesdays, and Fridays, Mr. Jones gets into his car and drives to his office, but on Tuesdays and Thursdays he boards a bus which transports him to his office).

Both approaches are goal-directed. But note that neither type of consistency is inherently superior to the other. In the example given here Mr. Jones gets to his office on time every day, either way. The only means by which a qualitative judgment could be made as to which type of consistency was superior would be to establish some criterion by which the two could be compared. The best technique would be the one that could be shown to act most effectively in helping the individual reach his desired goal. Only after establishing such a meaningful criterion could the individual decide on a rational basis just which form of consistency best served his own needs.

It is important that the distinction between these two different forms of consistency be made, because most parents are aware of the existence of fixed-response consistency only. Being unaware of any alternative, parents tend to be indiscriminately consistent in this one way. The danger is that when used to excess, fixed-response consistency creates excessive anger in spite of its potential usefulness in certain routine situations.

Let us look now at two typical situations that might confront a parent while the child is growing up: (1) On school nights a child's bedtime has been set at eight thirty P.M. One weekday evening, however, a one-hour television "special" made specifically for children is scheduled to appear beginning at nine P.M. The child pleads for permission to remain awake long enough to see the show. Following the rule of fixed-response consistency (bedtime is bedtime), the parent denies the child's repeated requests. (2) One morning a child complains of not feeling well. The mother checks all the obvious indicators, including the child's temperature, and finds them normal. To be conservative, however, she permits him to remain home from school. During the morning the child eats heartily and remains in good spirits. About noontime he asks permission to go into the living room in order to watch television. Later in the day, when he hears the other children returning home from school, he asks permission to go outside to play with them. The mother denies both requests. She admonishes the child for trying to "put one over" on her. She explains to the child: "This morning you told me that you were sick. Sick people do not have any fun. Sick people just stay in bed until they are well."

Why would a normally sensitive parent be likely to act so callously toward his child? Because, for the most part, he is aware of this one type of consistency only and he has been indoctrinated quite thoroughly to believe that it is the only correct and responsible way for a parent to behave. In contrast, if this mother had been aware of the alternative of variable-response consistency, she would have been willing to make exceptions to her rules. In the first case, she would have permitted the child to remain awake beyond his usual bedtime so that he could watch the television special. In the second case, so long as the child appeared to be in good health, she would have allowed him both to watch television in the living room and later to go outside to play. The use of variable-response consistency in these situations represents a far more humane approach to child-rearing than does the more rigid application of fixed-response consistency. However, to the extent that variable-response consistency is known at all, it is considered a form of inconsistency suitable for use only by weak-willed parents who lack the "guts" to be firm with their children.

Because of this, fixed-response consistency tends to be vastly overutilized in our society today. This principle is applied blindly and indiscriminately. Usually no significant effort is made by parents to determine its effectiveness by measuring it in terms of any meaningful criterion. One type of consistency is being practiced almost exclusively because of the traditional reverence accorded the term itself. Parents are acting consistently because "everyone knows" good parents act consistently.

I am suggesting now that parents reorient their thinking about consistency in two ways: First, recognize that there are two different types of consistency and that neither one is inherently superior to the other as a means of influencing children's behavior. Second, establish a definite goal and then with careful use of individual judgment decide which form of consistency seems most likely to enhance progress toward that goal (i.e., to help the child improve his behavior in the future).

If the reader will take these steps, he will find that there are times when one form of consistency will appear more promising than the other. The key to his decision will lie in the criterion he chooses by which to assess the effectiveness of either technique.

As the reader well knows by now, the criterion I want him to adopt is: How will my actions be likely to affect the status of the balance existing between the forces of love and the forces of anger within my child's personality?

This can be determined very readily at all times by applying the Golden Rule. Consider the cases of the two children described earlier in this chapter. How would the child have felt when his mother refused him permission to stay up later one night to watch a television program? Angry! How would the other child have felt when his mother refused him permission to go outside to play? Angry!

The important fact for parents to consider is this: When overutilized or used inappropriately, fixed-response consistency produces excessive degrees of anger. This is the major disadvantage of this type of consistency. Extensive clinical experience has demonstrated repeatedly that rigid, undeviating enforcement of specific standards, backed up by punishment or the threat of punishment, untempered by the discriminate use of compassion, gives the child the idea that the parents are sadistic and unloving. This idea is the precursor to emotional disturbances in children.

It appears to me that parents can fulfill their responsibilities to their children more completely by establishing as their primary goal the consistent manifestation of love as expressed through different or changing forms of behavior. This is consistency of a profoundly human order.

This idea may appear shockingly new or radical to parents. In reality the idea is quite venerable and conservative, although it was considered quite radical when it was first introduced approximately two thousand years ago. You will recall that Jesus kept getting himself in trouble with the established authorities by deviating from the formal written law when in his own judgment it was more humane to do so.

In the case of the woman taken in adultery, for example, fixed-response consistency dictated that she be stoned to death. This was the law. But Jesus responded to a higher order of law. He had the courage to manifest his compassion, to make an exception, that is, to utilize variable-response consistency. He forgave her with the simple instruction: "Neither do I condemn you; go and do not sin again." Jesus' consistency was shown in the uniformity with which his actions demonstrated love. Love was his criterion.

But Jesus did not claim credit for introducing this manner of expressing compassion toward one's fellows. Rather, when he permitted his followers to pick wheat on the Sabbath in order to assuage their hunger, he pointed out that David had made a similar kind of exception. He said, "The sabbath was made for man, not man for the sabbath."

Fixed sets of rules can fulfill a useful purpose. They may serve to guide a parent in approximately the right direction much of the time. In this way fixed sets of rules are completely desirable. But the parent must feel free to deviate from a rule, no matter how sound the rule in a majority of situations, if following the rule would be detrimental to his child's welfare. There is no way a parent can abdicate his responsibility for using independent judgment in raising his own children.

Many parents are fearful of assuming this burden of individual responsibility. They seek instead the comfort of "knowing" they are doing right by going "by the book." To these parents I offer this reassurance: Depending on your own judgment is not as difficult as you might imagine. All that is necessary is that you draw on the resources of your own Judeo-Christian heritage. Reflect on the Golden Rule and then (this is the only difficult part) have the courage to do what your own human feelings indicate should be done. Do not be afraid that your display of love through kindness will weaken or destroy your child's character.

I am not suggesting here that fixed-response consistency is a vice or that its use in everyday practice should be abandoned. Parental consistency will play an important role in teaching the child about many different aspects of the environment. There is an orderliness in the world, and parents have the responsibility for teaching children to respond effectively to this order. The intelligent response to this orderliness and predictability in the environment enables man to plan ahead wisely and thus to survive.

The universe appears to behave like a marvelously complex machine, and human beings function, in part, like exquisite little machines. It is the parents' responsibility to help the smaller machine function harmoniously with the larger one. But human beings are also more than machines, possessing some as yet undefinable quality that makes them different. Theologians historically have described this quality as a fragment of "the Divine Spirit" existing in all of us. Minority group members define approximately the same quality with the word "soul." To be lacking in "soul" is to be something less than human. Regardless of the name or the difficulty in defining it, almost everyone agrees that it exists in human beings.

Because of this quality, human beings demand of other human beings more than that they be treated as machines. One of the greatest sources of dissatisfaction in present-day societies is that the personal needs and feelings of the individual are either ignored or crushed under the weight of a technologically oriented, bureaucratically dominated society.

In a growing reaction against these powerful impersonal forces, people are beginning to insist that they be treated in ways that demonstrate consideration and respect for their basic human dignity and worth. In everyday affairs, this takes the form of their demanding to be treated with courtesy, understanding, and compassion by those holding power in the society.

Certainly, if the goal of parents is to enhance the feelings of closeness, warmth, and love existing between themselves and their children, it is necessary that they refrain from acting in ways which mimic those of the cold, impersonal, mechanistic, technological, and unforgiving society.

A great deal of the literature produced by our "alienated youth" today centers around feelings of loneliness. They complain about so many people feeling cut off from others, unable to establish any reassuring contact. Such writing usually is very critical of our mechanistic, technological society. They accuse the entire society of being cold, aloof, disinterested, and insensitive to the needs of the individual for warmth, affection, and a feeling of belonging.

These complaints, while poignant, are misdirected. It is impossible for an individual to relate in a warm, friendly, intimate, personal way to anything as large as an institution of the society. It is possible for one human being to relate warmly to another but not to an entire segment of the population. Although it may make excellent propaganda, it makes no sense to accuse General Motors or the Congress of the United States for the fact that several million people feel alienated because they are not having their individual needs for affection met by other people. The primary function of General Motors is to manufacture useful goods, safe for public use, and to sell them at a profit. The primary function of the Congress is to carry out its Constitutionally defined duties in governing the country. Neither of them has the responsibility nor the capacity for interacting with an individual human being so as to make him feel less lonely.

In our society the primary responsibility for producing feelings of love within the individual and thereby of helping to insulate him against feelings of loneliness and depression rests with those people who play the most prominent role during the "alienated" youth's formative years—his parents.

The young people today who are "screaming" loneliness and blaming the larger institutions of the organized society (i.e., the church, the school, capitalism) are really complaining about what they believe they failed to receive from their own parents. Society as a whole is merely being made the scapegoat while the real source of the difficulty, the events that took place while these children were growing up in their own homes, remains unidentified.

As long as parents persist in responding mechanistically to

their children, as dictated by the fixed-response-consistency approach, they will be in danger of producing still more alienated youth who will attack their society and its values when they are really angry with their own parents.

I hope now that the reader will be able to view the concept of consistency with greater perspective.

In the chapter following, I will present several illustrations of how I might advise parents to deal with certain forms of childish misbehavior. Knowing what you now know about the different kinds of consistency, the strategy underlying my recommendations should be more readily discernible to you.

10

HOW TO PUNISH
AND STILL BE LOVING

The following two cases illustrate different aspects of the approach to punishment that I have recommended to parents for use in various situations requiring it. In both of these cases, I describe how a particular parent dealt with a situation in accordance with the principles recommended here. While the actions of the parents may appear to be different in these illustrations, they will be similar in that all such behavior will be determined by the same underlying strategy. The parents are making practical application of the Golden Rule in order to enhance love and to minimize the child's irrational anger in situations that usually demand some form of punishment.

CASE NO. 1: Immediately preceding dinner time, a seven-year-old boy was disturbing three other family members. He kept getting in Mother's way, making it more difficult for her to prepare dinner. He persisted in teasing his sister, who was attempting to complete her homework. The noise of the repeated scolding and bickering was disturbing the father, who was trying to read his newspaper in peace after one hour's driving on a freeway. After having given repeated warnings, which the child ignored, the father angrily ordered the boy to his room for the remainder of the evening.

The father's action, while "solving" one problem, raised at least two others that night: (1) Since the child had been banished to his room before eating, what was to be done about his dinner? (2) The child had been anticipating watching a particular television "special" that night. What was to be done about that?

The parents handled the situation by having the mother take a tray of food to the child, who ate his dinner, alone, in his room, and later inviting the child out of his bedroom into the living room to watch the television program he had been anticipating. Then, after the program, he was sent back to his room to "finish" his punishment.

These parental actions, of course, violate the tenets of the traditional approach to child-rearing which would have demanded that the child be denied both his dinner and the television program in order to make his punishment more "meaningful" (i.e., painful). "What kind of punishment is that," a traditionalist would ask, "when the child is served dinner in his own room and then is invited out to enjoy himself by watching television?"

Here again, the reader can see that the traditional approach to child-rearing would demand one sequence of parental actions and my own approach another. The difference in approach hinges in large part on whether or not one is willing to give credence to the idea that a child who develops excessively angry feelings will display them, eventually, in some form of socially undesirable behavior.

In supporting the actions of the parents described in Case No. 1, my position is that a child who was left alone in his room, hungry, listening to the sounds of his family enjoying television in an adjoining room, would become very angry with his parents and his sister.

Being irrational, the child would use various devices for evading any sense of personal responsibility for creating his predicament. Rather, he would define himself as having been unjustly persecuted by his parents. He might even conclude that the parents had tricked him in some way so that they could lock him in his room and let his sister (whom they preferred) watch television alone.

The child's feeling of anger, generated by the parental punishment, would then combine with his paranoid misperception of himself as someone persecuted. The result would be to increase rather than decrease the probability that the child would behave improperly in the future. Angry feelings are reflected in angry behavior.

In contrast, the parents described in Case No. 1 used punishment discreetly and "softly," primarily as a symbolic gesture indicative of their disapproval of the child's actions in annoying the family. Their behavior in serving the child some dinner in his room and in permitting him to watch his preferred television program was designed, not to demonstrate the parental power to inflict pain, but rather as a means of enhancing love and of dissipating anger.

These parental actions make it very difficult for the child to cast the parents in the role of persecutors and himself in the role of the martyred victim. Such actions also make it very difficult for the child to deny his own responsibility by blaming the parents. The parental restraint manifested in refusing to apply a punishment of equal or greater magnitude than the child's original transgression creates an environment within the child in which conscience can grow. This is nothing more than has been taught in the Old and New Testaments for centuries.

Quite often, children who have not been punished to the extent that their own misbehavior might have warranted will ask for additional punishment. This is evidence that healthy guilt has been experienced. In such a situation the child might suggest, for example, that his father spank him, or "ground him" for an entire week, so as to "repay" the parents for letting him watch the television show.

The fact that a child may ask for punishment is often interpreted, mistakenly, as indicating that children have a "need for punishment." Advocates of this position argue that the child knows intuitively what is best for himself (i.e., punishment) and that the parents are doing him a favor by providing it for him. Indeed, they argue, if the parents withhold such punishment, they may do serious injury to the child's personality, because he might be forced to injure himself in order to atone for his own excessive guilt. "Help your child relieve his guilt," they say. Give him freedom through punishment.

This viewpoint fails woefully to grasp what is really going on inside the child. It serves primarily as a rationalization for parents who themselves have a "need to punish" but who do not wish to acknowledge the harshness and cruelty associated with their actions toward the child.

A child's request that he receive extra punishment suggests that some healthy guilt has been aroused. This provides the parents with an opportunity to do something constructive about the child's conscience development, but only if they are willing to withhold punishment.

The child's request for additional punishment indicates that the parents have created a healthy state of imbalance within the child between the opposing forces of his conscience (good) and his impulses (bad). The request for punishment indicates that the force of conscience, at that moment, has become stronger. It gained in strength because the parents, by withholding punishment, stripped the child of the use of his irrational defense against them and thereby against his own conscience.

Momentarily, at least, the child has been rendered incapable of using his favorite defense (i.e., "I am not bad, because they are bad also"). He is the only one in the situation who has been bad. Being deprived of his irrational defense mechanism by the parents' act of withholding punishment, the child is forced to look directly at the fact of his own "badness."

This direct confrontation is very painful to the child. But from the standpoint of the parents, the broader society, and, ultimately, the child also, this kind of pain is very desirable, because it acts as a driving force that produces growth of conscience.

The child, having been forced to look directly at his own "badness," will experience a particular kind of pain we call guilt. Pain, as we all know, is an unpleasant experience from which people normally strive to escape. The child, having experienced the pain of guilt, will inevitably try to do something to escape it. He will find that there exist two primary alternatives: (1) He may choose to undergo some other form of pain (i.e., punishment) as a substitute by means of which he purchases his freedom from the initial guilt he was experiencing. (2) He may choose to atone, to eliminate in the future the "bad" behavior that produced the guilt (pain) on this occasion. He relieves his current guilt by promising himself that he will be a "good boy" in the future. The second alternative, of course, is the healthier. Something takes place within the child that will help him to control his "bad" impulses in the future. This represents the restraining power of conscience which, in this one instance, is strengthened to some degree. The child himself decides to "be good" in order to avoid a form of pain (guilt) produced by himself. Except for the parents' having acted as catalysts to produce guilt, by the withholding of punishment, the entire issue of good vs. bad has been deposited just where it belongs: inside the child.

If the parents choose to punish the child's wrongdoing consistently, they become unwilling co-conspirators in an undertaking that can prevent the child from developing conscience indefinitely. The child was bad and he paid for it. The slate was wiped clean. He is now ready to misbehave again, and he will continue to endure some substitute pain for the more disturbing pain of guilt.

Following the parental application of punishment, the child reverts to his previous, nonconflictual, infantile level of conscience development. As before, he remains completely dependent for control over his antisocial impulses, not on any constructive force within himself, but solely on the power of fear of those in authority (parental or governmental) to inflict pain upon him. In the area of conscience development, the consistent use of punishment maintains him for his lifetime at the level of an infant.

On the other hand, if the parents can learn to withhold punishment, especially in those instances in which the child by logical standards has earned it, they will force the child to use the second alternative described above. That is, they will place the child in such a position that the only way he can eliminate his pain, the pain of guilt, will be through abandoning his wrongdoing.

As I have stated previously, the recommendations made in this book are based not so much on the discoveries of modern-day psychology as on the powerful and beautiful insights of our Judeo-Christian teachings. A brief review of the New Testament, for example, should convince the reader that many of my suggestions to parents consist of nothing more nor less than that they act toward their own children who misbehave in the same way that Jesus acted toward those around him who misbehaved.

According to various reports in the New Testament, Jesus came across many people who had acted reprehensibly. He acted toward them in certain ways, and they reformed. Certainly, those people who profess to believe in Jesus should be willing to follow the example he demonstrated to us so clearly how to act toward those who misbehave, so as to get them to change: A crippled man on a stretcher was placed before Jesus to be cured. Did Jesus berate him for his past sins? Did Jesus order him to be punished before he would be considered worthy of receiving a cure? No. Jesus said to him simply, "Your sins are forgiven." Peter denied Jesus three times, as Jesus had predicted. Is there any report in the New Testament that Jesus then castigated Peter or punished him in any way?

Jesus was not accomplishing his conversions and cures by means of his power to inflict pain. In all instances the constructive changes that occurred in people took place after Jesus withheld the use of punishment.

Clearly, if one believes the description of events in the New Testament, the Judeo-Christian heritage does not support the notion that a responsible parent must reprimand, reproach, vilify, and assault his own child in order to "raise him up in the way he should go."

Case No. 2: A nine-year-old girl was playing contentedly with some dolls when Mother intervened to inform her that it was bedtime. The child wanted to continue playing and did so in spite of repeated urging by the mother to "put the dolls away and get ready for bed." Finally, after the mother became very insistent, the child shouted angrily, "Well, all right then!" struck at her dolls and toy furniture, and scattered them about the floor of the room.

In spite of her own inner feelings of tension, the mother refrained from raising her voice to the same level as the child's. Neither did the mother begin screaming, scolding, and threatening. Rather, she tried to remain rational as the child gradually deteriorated to a more primitive level of functioning. Even after the child had scattered her toys recklessly across the bedroom floor, the mother did not react with shock and horror as if she had suddenly discovered that her child was "possessed."

As calmly as she could, the mother helped the child to pick up the dolls and to put them away neatly. She did not create a second opportunity for conflict by ordering the child to "pick up those toys right now, young lady, or else." When a parent asserts herself in this way, it may be momentarily reassuring as an overt demonstration that she is in complete control of the situation. The child, however, being forced to pick up the dolls, being forced to act out overtly her subordinate relationship to the mother, would only develop more intense anger which further complicates the parent-child relationship later.

After the mother had helped the child put away the dolls, the child continued to pout as she prepared herself for bed. When she was under the covers (finally) the mother entered the bedroom, as was her custom, hugged the child warmly, kissed her good night and said: "Honey, I'm sorry you had such a hard time tonight. I know how much children hate to go to bed, especially when they're having so much fun playing."

The child's response was to break out in tears, throw her arms around the mother and say, "Oh, Mommy, I'm so sorry."

This statement from the child and the child's embrace of the mother indicated that the mother had achieved her primary objectives:

1. She had aroused loving feelings within the child. She had undermined irrational anger. In so doing, she had stripped the child of her irrational defenses against accepting blame for her own misbehavior.

2. This made possible the arousal of the child's conscience. This is the force which acts to compete with or inhibit further expressions of childish, antisocial impulses.

Throughout this book I have attempted to demonstrate how it is that during the normal process of child-rearing, consistent parental retaliation for childish misbehavior brings about a damaging separation between a young person and his parents. Now, however, if you will examine the two cases presented thus far in this chapter, you will observe that the outcome of these unhappy situations can be altered. In each case the situation that began with the child having done something wrong, something normally demanding parental disapproval or punishment, ended with the parent and the child becoming even closer and more loving than before. This is the advantage of the technique I am recommending to parents.

In contrast, the simple administration of punishment does not accomplish this. It merely creates separation, conflict, and misunderstanding among family members. This is the media in which delinquency flourishes.

Many parents would define the actions of the child described in Case No. 2 as a temper tantrum. "After all," they would say, "the child was very disagreeable and she did scatter her dolls on the bedroom floor." These parents would argue that by treating the child with kindness, by helping her to pick up the dolls and withholding severe punishment, the mother had condoned the child's misbehavior. According to this line of reasoning, the mother's actions contributed to spoiling the child, thus making it more likely that the child would have temper tantrums in the future.

In my opinion, both the criticism of the mother and the idea that she was spoiling her child are incorrect.

These fears of spoiling the child in the temper-tantrum situation are based primarily on a misunderstanding of a basic principle of human learning—the reinforcement principle. The reason for this misunderstanding stems from the fact that parents fail to recognize the crucial distinction between (1) accepting (or tolerating) a particular form of behavior and (2) rewarding that particular form of behavior.

Most parents believe, erroneously, that allowing a form of behavior to occur without punishing it is synonymous with rewarding it. In reality there is a significant difference between the two. This difference, when understood properly, dictates different forms of parental behavior in order for the parent to attain his objective.

To make this distinction more meaningful to parents, let us digress briefly and examine a relatively simple situation in which the principles involved might be clearly demonstrated.

Very often, in studying the behavior of living organisms, a psychologist will confine a small animal—a cat, for example—in a box. The box will contain a movable lever, which the cat can manipulate, and an empty food tray. If the psychologist wants the cat to learn to press the bar, he will connect the lever with a mechanical feeder in such a way that every time the cat presses the lever, a small amount of cat food will be deposited into the food tray. Once this connection is made, the cat, gradually and over a period of time, learns to press the lever in order to provide itself food. The psychologist would observe that the cat's lever-pressing behavior occurred more and more frequently as long as it was rewarded with the receipt of the expected food. The reward (food) served the purpose of reinforcing the behavior (bar-pressing).

Now, suppose the psychologist decided to stop the cat from pressing the lever. All that would be necessary would be for him to disconnect the lever from the automatic food dispenser. Thereafter, when the cat pressed the lever, it would fail to receive its anticipated food reward. After a relatively brief period of time, the cat would stop pressing the lever. A psychologist would say that the lever-pressing behavior had been "extinguished." In this situation the withholding of the reward (food) weakened the behavior in question (lever-pressing) to the point that it disappeared. Pressing the lever, when it occurred, was accepted or tolerated. At no time was it necessary to punish the animal when it pressed the lever in order for the response to be eliminated!

As you can see, both the psychologist-animal and the parent-child relationships contain essentially the same elements: (1) a pliable subject (child or animal), (2) behaving in some particular way (lever-pressing or temper tantrum), (3) being manipulated by a more powerful, controlling person (psychologist or parent) who is (4) regulating the dispensation or the withholding of rewards valued by the subject (food or playtime).

Let us look again at the behavior of the mother in Case No. 2. Was she guilty of increasing the probability that her daughter's temper tantrums would increase in frequency? The answer is NO! And why? Because the mother was not rewarding the child's behavior, she was merely accepting or tolerating it without administering a punishment. What the child wanted was more playtime. This constituted the reward in the situation. As long as the mother did not give the child more playtime as a direct consequence of the tantrum, she was not rewarding the offensive behavior.

This would be comparable to the actions of the psychologist who was trying to "extinguish" the lever-pressing response. It was not necessary that he do something, such as punishing the animal every time the animal pressed the lever. All that was required to eliminate the undesired response was to withhold the food reward.

As long as the mother withheld the reward that the child desired (i.e., more playtime), she was training the child as well and as effectively as the psychologist who was eliminating the lever-pressing response of the cat in the laboratory.

The mother's actions in speaking kindly, in withholding punishment, and in helping the child to pick up the toys did not constitute a reward, because they did not provide the child with the ultimate goal of the tantrum—more playtime. These parental actions, however, did serve a very important function in the parent-child relationship. They reduced the intensity of irrational anger in the child initiated by the legitimate parental request and they served to enhance the feelings of love existing between the child and her mother. The mother's restraint provided the soil for the loving reconciliation that would occur after the irrational anger of the child had subsided.

Of course there are many who would insist that the animal (or the child) would learn to eliminate a nondesired response more quickly if punishment was introduced into the learning process. They might argue, for example, that if the psychologist had administered a mild electric shock, in addition to merely withholding food when the animal pressed the lever, the cat would have desisted more quickly from that action.

This is a very tempting line of reasoning. The only thing wrong with it is that clinical experience and experimental evidence suggest that just the opposite is true.

Experimental research with animals has shown that when punishment is used to eliminate a particular response, the punished response does not really disappear. Rather, it is suppressed temporarily, only to return in its original form and strength once the animal discovers that punishment is being withheld. Furthermore, many experiments with animals have shown that the use of punishment as a deterrent has many undesirable side effects. In response to punishment as a teaching device, animals will show signs of behavioral disturbances that resemble very closely neurotic or psychotic reactions in human beings.

But even if a parent were relatively unimpressed by the available clinical and experimental evidence, I believe his own sense of fair play could define for him the most suitable manner of reacting to children's temper tantrums.

How many ways are available to children in our complex, highly organized society for expressing feelings of anger? The demands of civilized living on a crowded planet are so great as to permit virtually no socially acceptable outlet. Children are not permitted (and rightly so, of course) to hit or to speak disrespectfully to adults. Even fighting with other children constitutes a basis for disciplinary action at school and in the neighborhood. They are not permitted to defy the rules set up by those in authority (again rightly so). They are not permitted to destroy personal property. They are not permitted to use "foul" language and they are not permitted to display, overtly, evidence that suggests anger (i.e., Wipe that look off your face, young man, or I'll wipe it off for you!).

Even the vicarious enjoyment of anger is gradually being restricted. For example, many parents will not permit their children to watch enactments of violence portrayed on television and in the movies. There is even a movement developing to prevent children from playing in games or with toys (i.e., guns) that reflect "real" violence. Thus, even symbolic or disguised expressions of hostility are becoming "taboo."

Would it not be simply a matter of fair play and common decency for parents to permit their children to "blow off some steam" in a periodic display of temper which (1) harmed no one and (2) gained the child no tangible reward except the feeling of relief at having expressed, very forcefully, a strong emotion?

In view of what is already known about the undesirable effects of constant punishment, my advice to parents on the subject of temper tantrums is as follows: Tolerate them. Permit them to take place, without resorting to threats and punishment. Make certain only that you have identified correctly the reward the child is seeking to gain through his tantrums and make sure that he does not obtain it by means of the tantrum. Do not fear being kind to the child during and after the time he is having the tantrum. Do not refrain from making friendly gestures toward the child during and after the time he puts on his emotional display. Remember, it is not necessary for you to convince the child that you detest his behavior in order to eliminate it. All that is necessary is that the child not be rewarded for it.

Parents who follow these guidelines will find that their children's temper tantrums gradually will occur less frequently and eventually will disappear entirely. Of equal importance, the balance in the child's "love bank" will be far healthier than it might otherwise be if the parent permitted all instances of the child's display of temper to become occasions for parent-child warfare.

11

GUIDELINES ON THE
USE OF PUNISHMENT

The following recommendations, which summarize the advice given in the previous chapters on punishment, are designed to (1) make punishment more effective as a training device while (2) avoiding the production of undesirable side effects such as bad feelings between family members, juvenile delinquency, and drug addiction:

1. Avoid the use of disapproval, scolding, threats, and punishment whenever it is reasonably possible to do so.

2. When it becomes necessary to punish, make the punishment as mild as is reasonably possible. Use it primarily for its symbolic value rather than for the supposedly "therapeutic" value of pain itself.

3. Anticipate the possible future course of parent-child interaction once a punishment is initiated. Try to avoid becoming enmeshed in conflict situations that are self-perpetuating, demanding ever more severe applications of punishment.

4. Don't insist on too wide a range of "good" behavior that the child, for biologically determined reasons, is unable to produce. Make a distinction between those forms of behavior which are vital to the child's (or others') welfare and those which are merely "nice." Reserve the use of disapproval and punishment for those behaviors you have defined as vital.

5. Try to avoid punishing the child for failing to perform routine tasks, such as chores, at levels of efficiency attainable only

by mature adults. Children, because of their biologically determined immaturity, must inevitably reveal traits of undependability, carelessness, poor judgment, impulsiveness, and disorganization. No amount of punishment can change what nature has created, prior to maturation.

6. Temper your punishment with compassion. At times offer overt signs of love, rather than punishment, to the child who has just committed some misdeed.

7. Recognize that getting a child to behave properly, even in an area of vital concern, will take time, patience, and flexibility. No punishment yet invented has been shown capable of producing instant obedience.

A parent using these seven points as guidelines would not be abdicating his responsibility toward the child in any way. Note that I do not suggest that the parent desist from attempting to teach the child the difference between right and wrong; I do not recommend that the parent refrain completely from lecturing, scolding, reprimanding, or threatening the child on certain occasions; and I do not recommend that parents abandon the use of punishment in various forms on certain occasions. Because parents are dealing with a basically irrational organism, punishment will always remain as one important teaching device. At times it will be the only effective technique available. However, I do encourage parents to adopt an attitude of moderation in their use of discipline and punishment. This means that they must use punishment with the degree of restraint that good judgment and mercy would require.

Extensive clinical experience has proven to me the value of the seven principles listed at the beginning of this chapter. This same experience, however, has also proven to me that parents are difficult to convince. I wish to review here certain objections that are raised by parents, typically, about my recommendations and, if possible, to put to rest these objections with some additional case histories.

The objections might be summarized roughly as follows: (1) Your approach takes too long to produce the desired behavior in the child. Surely, if the parent introduced strong punishment early enough and forcefully enough, he could get the child to conform more quickly. (2) I observe that the neighbors' children are very polite, well-groomed, and perform their chores regularly as well. If their children can perform reliably and responsibly, biological limitations must have nothing to do with it. It must be a simple matter of discipline. If their children can behave that way, why can't mine?

I will attempt to answer the first objection, "Your approach takes too long . . . ," with the following case history:

The parents of a fifteen-year-old girl became concerned when their daughter developed consistently negativistic, rebellious, and uncooperative actions both at home and at school. Her grades dropped markedly. She acted defiantly toward her teachers. She had been punished in various ways at school and had been expelled several times for such behavior as using "foul" language, smoking on the school grounds, and disrupting classroom activities. At home, she violated many family rules by failing to come home promptly after school, etc.

During a conference with the school authorities, the parents discovered that their daughter's pattern of misbehavior had begun at approximately the same time she had become a very close friend of one girl who also had been acting quite rebelliously.

These parents were very responsible people. They had been reading up on the problem of juvenile delinquency and they had attended several lectures on the subject. The advice they had received on the subject could best be summarized with a brief quote from an article written by Art Linkletter. Mr. Linkletter, as you probably know, experienced a great personal tragedy when his "youngest daughter Diane took her own life in a mood of irrationality, panic and despair that was the aftermath of a bad trip on LSD" (*Reader's Digest,* February, 1970). Following the death of his daughter, Mr. Linkletter has devoted considerable effort toward helping other parents to protect their children against the "plague" of drug abuse.

Mr. Linkletter's advice in the *Reader's Digest* article consisted, in part, of the following statement: "Talk to your family doctor if you become seriously alarmed. Ask yourself if you are being too permissive. If so, tighten up on discipline. As long as your child is a minor, living at home, you are his first line of defense, even against himself. Don't let the fear of alienating him make you duck your responsibilities."

The parents decided that the first step in rehabilitating their daughter would be to forbid her from having any further contact with the "bad influence." They were, of course, acting conscientiously to follow the advice put out for parents by many civic-minded organizations: "Know who your child's associates are and do your duty to protect him against the undesirable element."

The parents could not realize it at the time, but they had begun a long campaign that would escalate uncontrollably, once initiated.

At first they simply forbade their daughter to associate with the delinquent girl friend. Appropriate threats of punishment were made concerning possible violations of the parental injunction.

The daughter, however, continued to meet her friend surreptitiously. When discovered periodically by the parents, the daughter was punished not only for violating the parents' orders (which she had been warned about) but additionally for lying about her contacts.

As the parents became more aware of the subterfuges to which their daughter would resort, they began to supervise her more closely. For example, they insisted that she give them the name of the friend to whose home she said she was going. The mother would later verify the daughter's presence at the home with a telephone call.

The increased parental supervision, of course, resulted in the child's devising more sophisticated means for seeing her friend, and thereby escaping detection. A conspiracy was established whereby a friend acceptable to the parents would telephone and invite the daughter over. The mother would give her consent. Meanwhile, the acceptable friend would have invited the unacceptable girl friend over, also.

Each time that the daughter was discovered to have violated the parents' "trust" she was reprimanded, punished, and restricted more severely. The father, in anger, began using words like "tramp," "whore," and "slut."

The daughter had already been deprived of her record player and her television privileges. For a time, her phone calls had been monitored. Then she lost her phone privileges entirely. She had been restricted to the home for longer and longer periods until finally a rule was established that she was to go nowhere except to school, at any time, unless accompanied by one of the parents. Periodically, also, she had been given an "old-fashioned thrashing."

Ultimately, the daughter decided to use a very ancient ruse. She would retire for the night as she was supposed to. She would then arrange her pillows to resemble a body asleep in bed. Then, after she was reasonably certain that her parents were asleep, she would escape out of her bedroom window. This, when discovered, was the occasion for the harshest punishment ever administered to the child. Following this, the daughter attempted suicide.

At that point, the parents sought professional help.

In reviewing the case history data, I found that the parents, at all times, had acted toward the daughter in ways that they believed to be best for her character development. They had administered all the socially sanctioned forms of pain available to parents. Obviously, in this case, the old way did not work. This case is not at all an exception.

There is no "speedy" way to train children to behave properly. What appears to be rapid training must always depend on the fear of pain, and fear of pain achieves only one end: it empties the "love bank," setting the stage for later difficulty.

The second parental objection I wish to comment upon is: "The neighbors' children are very polite. . . . If their children can behave that way, why can't mine?"

Every family seems to have at least one neighbor "up the street" whose children are models of decorum. These children are always well scrubbed and neatly dressed. They speak respectfully to their parents and other adults, and they do their chores regularly and cheerfully. At least, this is the way it appears.

I am convinced that this hypothetical child up the street is a myth, a myth that would be readily shattered if the outside observer had any real insight into what was going on inside the neighbors' home and inside the child.

A great many of the emotionally disturbed children who are brought to my office because of the presenting symptoms of negativism, rebelliousness, etc., have a prior history of having been exceptionally well behaved children. Moreover, a great many of my adult patients, people suffering debilitating disorders such as alcoholism, drug addiction, and severe depression, had been, as children, exceptionally well behaved and obedient. Undoubtedly, many of these people were the "good children . . . up the street" whom other parents were admiring so and wishing their own children would emulate.

One of my patients, a woman in her late forties who had spent ten years of her adult life in a sanitarium because of severe depression, gave me the following vignette of her childhood experiences:

"Sunday was visiting day. Mother would dress up all the children very beautifully. Whenever we went to see Mr. and Mrs. _____, Father would sit all four of the children on a piano bench, arranged according to our height. I was the youngest, so naturally I sat on the end. He would warn us sternly not to get off the bench and not to get into mischief. Everyone always commented on how cute we looked sitting there in a row with our Sunday-best clothes on. They always said we made a beautiful picture. Sometimes Mrs. _____ would go next door and bring in other neighbors just to look at us. You can be sure we didn't move off that bench or speak until Father told us to, because we all knew what would happen to us if we did."

My patient, as I said, was chronically depressed as an adult.

How did her three brothers fare as adults? One had ulcers; one became alcoholic; and one committed suicide. This is not an isolated case. Any therapist in this country could produce dozens of similar illustrative cases from his own files.

But the average parent need not depend solely on the files of psychologists to provide such examples. Many similar cases become public knowledge when, because a serious crime is involved, they warrant the attention of the mass media. How many times during the past few years have you read about some very nice young man or woman who, one day, either commits suicide or picks up a gun or an ax and (apparently without provocation) murders a large number of people, often including all available members of his own immediate family?

Typically, the news reports in such cases describe the neighbors' reactions to the young person's act of violence as one of amazement. As far as the neighbors knew, the parents of the murderer had always been very respectable members of the community; they were somewhat stern with their child, but never unfair in administering punishment. Neither the father nor the child was in the habit of using profanity. As a matter of fact, the father would not "abide" the use of profanity by the child.

Prior to committing the suicide or the murders, the young man or woman had always been polite, well-mannered, obedient, and respectful toward adults. He or she was one of the very few young people in town who still addressed adults with the deferential "Yes, sir" or "Yes, ma'm." He or she was also a dedicated member of organized groups such as the local church and the Scouts, which inculcate the highest ethical ideals of our society.

The following article appeared in the *Los Angeles Herald-Examiner*, Tuesday, February 16, 1971:

"On Saturday morning, while his mother and father slept, [Jeff], our beloved son, took his life. His mother and dad appeal to all young people—if you know of any person . . . involved in illegal drug traffic, please turn their name or names in to proper authorities.

"[Jeff] was found in the basement by his mother. The youth had filled a galvanized pail with water, pulled a piano stool near after carefully rolling up his pants cuffs. . . . He put his feet in the water and then either grasped a live wire or turned on the current. He had fallen from the stool and lay on the floor where he was found.

" 'We suspect LSD,' " said his father. . . . 'If he'd just once said, "Dad, I need help" or "Mom, I need help." . . . But he never did.'

"Jeff seemed an unlikely victim of drugs: a 'Life' Boy Scout, co-captain of the wrestling team at _____ High School, a lifeguard during the summer, winner of the Sportsmanship Award from the town swimming club in 1970. His parents were extremely active in community affairs."

The parents arranged to have reports read of their son's suicide in two local churches to "quite possibly prevent another life from being destroyed."

Here is an excerpt from an article that appeared in the *Los Angeles Times,* September 1, 1971. It is about Charles Watson, one of the convicted killers involved in the bizarre Tate–LaBianca murders:

"Under examination by defense Attorney, Sam Bubrich, Mrs. Watson said that her son was an outstanding athlete and student at Farmersville High School . . . 'and he was voted the class favorite, belonged to the Spanish Club, was sports editor of the paper, a yell leader, had a part in the senior play, won a prize for play writing and was an honor student. He always went out to be best . . . and almost always was.' He was a member of the 4-H Club, Future Farmers of America and the Boy Scouts. He liked to go to church. . . . She said she and her husband operated a little general store and gas station. 'If it hadn't been for the boy helping out . . . we couldn't have run it.' "

And here is an excerpt from an article that appeared in the *Los Angeles Times*, February 2, 1971, concerning Patricia Krenwinkel. Miss Krenwinkel is one of the young women convicted recently of having participated in the gruesome Tate–LaBianca murders.

Miss Krenwinkel's parents reported to the *Times* staff writer:
"Her childhood was typically middle-class: church, Sunday School, Halloween trick or treating, Easter egg hunts, and the usual girlhood organizations. They said their daughter was a good baby, was never a behavior problem, and that she was gentle, loved animals, sang in the church choir, went to summer Bible School, taught the Bible, liked religion, and was never hostile, violent, or disrespectful.

" 'Did she cause you any trouble or grief as a child?' asked Paul Fitzgerald (Miss Krenwinkel's Attorney).

" 'Never,' said Krenwinkel. 'I couldn't have asked for a better one.'

"Miss Krenwinkel, 23, is the only Defendant among the four on trial who the prosecution claims actively participated in all seven Tate–LaBianca killings."

I ask the reader again to consider the evidence. Does it seem reasonable to suppose that Miss Krenwinkel's parents, who saw to it that she went to summer Bible school and who taught her to be obedient, respectful, nonhostile, and nonviolent, were the kind of parents who indulged their daughter by being overly permissive?

The sudden "personality change" in such young people is so startling and unbelievable that the neighbors attempt to explain it by reintroducing a modern-day form of demonology. They say such things as: "Drugs must have made her go crazy," or "He must have had some horrible tumor that disintegrated his brain."

This theorizing about drugs and tumors, of course, protects all concerned from the necessity for dealing with a very painful reality. This nice young man or nice young lady killed a lot of people because he or she was very, very angry. And, if he or she was very, very angry, someone, no matter how well-intentioned, must have made him or her very, very angry.

Acceptance of this fact would necessarily demand a reassessment of some long-esteemed ideas about child-rearing. But, such reassessment would also have to be quite painful. And, as we already know, people do not seem inclined to seek out painful experience.

It seems to me that parental efforts to produce model children, fully as obedient and dependable as the neighbors', are being carried out at too great a cost to the child and to society.

Unfortunately many children come to be used as nothing more than pawns in a contest conducted covertly by parents to enhance their own pride. The winner of the contest, the one who wins the "best parent" award, is the one who can produce a child who can be revealed publicly to be the most obedient, the most polite, the most well groomed, the best behaved at church, etc.

According to the unofficial rules of this competition, a parent who must issue a command twice is thought of less highly than one who has to issue an order only once. But neither is esteemed as much as a parent who can assure instant compliance with his wishes—with nothing more than an "icy" stare.

A majority of my alcoholic patients were controlled, as children, by the icy stare which derived its power for control on an extended, previous history of severe punishment.

It is time now that parents withdraw from this type of competition for personal ego-satisfaction. The proper test of good parenthood rests not in demonstrating the ability to produce immediate obedience in public, but rather in demonstrating the ability to raise an emotionally healthy, drug-resistant adult for the future. Parents who go to extraordinary lengths to produce perfect little ladies and gentlemen, at too great a cost to the child's health, should not be revered for their efforts. Similarly, parents who are willing to tolerate the normal imperfections of childhood, without abusing the children for them, should receive greater acceptance and approval. This will make the parents' job easier and help the children in the long run.

Of course, I am not suggesting that all or even most children who are obedient, dependable, polite, and perfectionistic, in the manner of adults, are in the process of developing a psychological disorder. The majority of children in our society will learn to conform, without experiencing excessive and destructive hostility. Millions of young people will be polite, obedient, etc., and grow up to be fine adults. However, I am trying to alert parents in the average middle-class American home to the fact that the primary source of danger for their child lies not in underregulation (permissiveness), as is commonly believed, but in overregulation. I wish to caution parents concerning these dangers so that they do not become awestruck at what appears to be a triumph over nature—revealed in the good behavior of the neighbors' children.

It might very well be the case that the surface picture of superb conformity in the neighbors' child is being purchased at too great a cost to the child, in a way that will be manifested only years later during the teen-age or young adult periods. In the long run, the less well organized, more naturally childlike child is emotionally healthier and less likely to turn to the use of drugs than the overly polite, overly obedient child who is a showpiece for his parents in the neighborhood.

One other objection that parents raise to my recommendations is this: "The approach you are suggesting sounds good but it seems to create the need for a great deal of hard work for the parents, especially for the mother."

I have no rebuttal for this assessment of the situation. Being a good parent does require hard work. The role of good-parenthood is as demanding as any other significant profession which can be undertaken in life.

Unfortunately, no formalized means has ever existed for teaching what should be known about this profession. All that has ever been required is a sperm, an egg, and the initiative to bring them together. Largely owing to the absence of a significant body of knowledge and the means for transmitting such knowledge to new parents (except through "old wives' tales"), the complexity of the parental role has been very poorly understood. The role of the parent has been both degraded and oversimplified.

In the extreme, the entire role of the parent has been reduced to one simple reflex response that completely eliminates the need for using any of the higher centers of cerebral activity. This response could be described as, "Swat 'em one if they step out of line." With the exception of the forearm muscle, this approach eliminates most of the "work" of parenthood.

But, as I have stated repeatedly in this book, the average middle-class parent does not rely excessively on the use of physical force as a training device. Rather, he oversimplifies the parental role by concentrating most of his training efforts on verbal reprimands, lectures, scolding, dirty looks, and more subtle forms of punishment than merely "swatting" the child. While not so primitive as the purely "physical" approach, the excessive dependence on the use of disapproval is nevertheless reflexive and in its own way eliminates the need for parental thought and work.

Often, after parents have discovered that their child has become a habitual drug user, they will plead: "Doctor, we'll do anything. *Anything at all* to help the child. Just tell us what to do to get him off drugs."

Unfortunately, by that time it is often too late, and there is nothing the parents can do that would help.

The suggestions I am making describe those things which the parents can do before the child becomes delinquent and goes on drugs and which will help ensure that he does not become delinquent. Of course, these recommendations will require hard work on the part of the parents. There are no shortcuts. But there is no point in waiting until after the child becomes drug-dependent before the parents begin to expend the effort required to handle their child in a therapeutic manner. What better way for a parent to demonstrate his love, overtly to the child, than through doing the hard work required of being a good parent?

12

GUIDELINES ON THE DEMANDS OF CHILDREN

As any parent knows, the requests and demands of children are infinite. Dealing with these repetitive demands creates as much difficulty for parents as does the issue of punishment.

The parent hates to say "No" all the time. But reality dictates that the parent cannot gratify every request made by the child. The painful issue confronting the parent is this: To what extent can the needs and desires of the child be gratified without "spoiling" him, without rendering him too "soft" to deal effectively with the routine frustrations of everyday life?

These are the guidelines I recommend in order to deal effectively with this difficult aspect of child-rearing:

1. Gratify the child's requests and satisfy or permit him to satisfy his needs whenever it is reasonable to do so. In brief, say "Yes" to the child whenever humanly possible.

2. Never deny a request or frustrate a child's needs because of an arbitrary reason unrelated to some practical or sensible consideration connected with the objective situation.

3. When the commonsense demands of reality make it necessary to deny a child's request or to block the satisfaction of a need, the parent should do so in the manner best calculated to protect the closeness of the parent-child relationship.

The use of all three principles is dictated by one basic consideration: they operate to enhance love and to reduce anger, particularly irrational anger.

In Chapter 1 of this book, I pointed out that parents become the objects of very strong feelings from their children, because the parents control, to a very great extent, the degree of pleasure or pain the child will experience while he is growing up. The differential distribution of this pleasure or pain will be regulated largely by the manner in which the parent deals with the issue of either gratifying or preventing the gratification of the child's needs. Also, the reader will recall that in Chapter 2, I described several aspects of the irrational functioning of the child's mind. One of these was that a child experiences some degree of anger every time one of his needs or desires is frustrated, in spite of the obvious logical necessity for the frustration imposed.

By gratifying the child's needs whenever reasonably possible, by avoiding the arbitrary imposition of frustration, and by saying "No" to the child only in certain diplomatic ways, parents should be able, constantly, to keep this irrational anger within safe limits. By expressing the proper kind of attitude while denying a child's requests, the parent may even be able to enhance the parent-child relationship. This, of course, is the ultimate goal of the parent, to enable the forces of love to triumph over the irrational forces at work in the child's mind.

This principle, as stated, was: "Gratify the child's requests and satisfy or permit him to satisfy his needs whenever it is reasonable to do so. In brief, say 'Yes' to the child whenever humanly possible."

The use of the word "reasonably" of course admits of considerable variation among parents. Different sets of parents will hold divergent opinions as to just what should be considered reasonable. But these differences are not so great as one might imagine and they tend to occur in a certain, select area of child-rearing, that area having to do with what might be referred to as morality, character-building, or taste.

On issues pertaining to the child's physical health and safety, there is widespread agreement among parents as to what is reasonable. Probably all parents would agree to frustrate their child's desires (and rightly so) if the child wanted to run out onto a busy thoroughfare, eat sweets to the exclusion of other foods, stay home from school indefinitely although not ill, hurt other children, destroy other people's property, etc.

It is in the areas of taste, character-building, or morality that significant differences between parental opinions are likely to occur. Parental judgments in these areas are not related to the child's immediate health, well-being, or safety, but seem to reflect more the parents' desires to make the child grow up to become a virtuous person of good taste and breeding in accordance with the parents' own conception of good taste and breeding.

The differences existing between parents in these areas will result in children of different families being exposed to wide variations in the amount of frustration that each, respectively, will be made to endure. Obviously, children of parents who define what is "reasonable" within very narrow limits must endure significantly greater amounts of frustration than children of parents who define the word "reasonably" more broadly.

One can deduce from this quite readily why it is that children of the most conscientious, the most responsible, the most organized, and the most reliable parents will experience the greatest share of frustration.

The central thesis of this book is that such frustration, when excessive, creates excessive anger, which in turn is expressed overtly in various forms of delinquency.

My recommendations to parents, then, are based on the idea that in order to reduce anger and delinquency, parents should apply the broadest possible interpretation that they can to what they would consider "reasonable" gratification for the child.

The word "reasonable" admittedly is lacking in scientific precision. I should like to attempt to define it and thus make it more meaningful to parents by means of brief excerpts from "real life" situations.

The following case history vignettes illustrate situations in which the parents were blocking the satisfaction of the child's needs or desires, in my opinion, unreasonably. The cases presented are meant to be suggestive rather than exhaustive.

SITUATION: A teen-age girl decides that her new eyeglasses should be of the type currently popular with girls her age. These glasses consist of circular lenses, encased in narrow, wire frames.

Her mother prefers the more elliptically shaped lenses encased in tinted plastic frames. These are the type the mother herself wears. She believes they are more practical and more becoming for a young girl, and she insists upon buying this style for her daughter.

The mother defends her actions as reasonable because: "I am the child's mother and I know what is best for my child," and, "It is my money which is being spent and therefore I have the right to make the final decision."

SITUATION: A twelve-year-old girl wants to telephone the boy in whom she is currently interested. She is alarmed because he seems to be ignoring her in favor of another girl at school.

The mother forbids her telephoning the boy.

The mother defends her actions as reasonable because: "When I was that age, nice young ladies did not telephone boys. It is a boy's place to telephone a girl."

SITUATION: A fifteen-year-old girl wants to wear her hair long so that it falls forward partly obscuring the face. It is a hair style common among teen-agers in her community, one that is accepted without question by the local school authorities. The parents insist vehemently, however, that the daughter wear her hair back, so that her face is always fully revealed.

The parents justify the reasonableness of their ruling as follows: (1) "We know that you are a nice girl, but the neighbors who do not know you as well might think you were not very nice if they saw you wearing that hair style." (2) "We think you have such a pretty face. We want everyone to be able to see it and enjoy it."

SITUATION: A group of mothers are sitting around one morning having a friendly conversation. They have sent their youngsters, ages two and one half to four and one half, into an adjoining room to play. One of the children, two and one half years old, returns to the room while the adults are talking, and without speaking lays her body across the mother's lap. The mother at first begins to stroke the child's back, gently, but then orders the child out of the room when the other mothers laugh and criticize her for "giving in" and spoiling the child.

SITUATION: A mother takes her eleven-year-old daughter shopping for shoes. While in the store, the daughter sees some high, tight, shiny plastic boots made for children her age. The child expresses an interest in owning such boots.

The mother refuses her request on the grounds that (1) "You would look silly in them" and (2) "There's time enough for that sort of thing later on." (Only years later will the child discover what the phrase "that sort of thing" meant. It expressed the mother's concern that the purchase of the skintight boots would have set the daughter, prematurely, on the road to sexual promiscuity.)

SITUATION: A sixteen-year-old girl wants to have a birthday party at her home for a boy in whom she is currently interested. The father refuses her the use of the home for the party. The reason given for the father's decision is that he does not approve of her boyfriend.

SITUATION: A mother is accompanying her six-year-old son on a "trick or treat" expedition one Halloween evening. At one of the homes on the way, the resident holds out to the child a basket filled with candy. The child digs into the basket and grasps two pieces. The mother makes him return one of them in spite of the resident's assurances that the child's taking two pieces was completely acceptable. The mother explains the reason for her action: "A child must learn proper manners. If I didn't teach him such things, who would? The fact that the woman who offered him the candy didn't object to his taking two pieces doesn't make it right."

SITUATION: The parent buys a young child a gas-filled balloon at an amusement park. Fulfilling his obligation as a parent, he warns the child, "Now don't let go of it or it will fly into the sky, and we won't be able to catch it." Inevitably, of course, at some point during the day, the child gets distracted and *lets go of the balloon,* which promptly ascends into the sky. The child cries bitterly and begs for another balloon. The parent refuses, however, because: "I warned you what would happen if you let it go. You will just have to learn to take better care of your things."

SITUATION: In an ice-cream parlor one day, a seven-year-old child orders a strawberry ice-cream cone because this is what his friend orders. His mother informs him that he has never liked strawberry ice cream. The child insists, so the mother orders the strawberry cone. When the child samples it, he finds, as Mother predicted, that he doesn't like it. The child asks for another cone. The mother denies his request in order to teach him a lesson. "Next time I tell you something, you'll listen to me."

SITUATION: A seven-year-old boy one day helps his father to wash the family car. The following day the child asks his father to go out with him and wash it again. The father declines, explaining to the son that they had washed the car the day before. (The father missed the point. The child just wanted to be with him.)

SITUATION: A mother is on a routine shopping trip to the supermarket. The child sees an inexpensive toy he wants. The mother turns down the request, explaining, (1) "You don't need that piece of junk," and (2) "You have a whole closet full of toys at home you never play with anyhow."

SITUATION: A twelve-year-old boy comes home one day and announces his intention of becoming a great tennis player. He asks his father to buy him a new tennis racket. The father refuses. He explains to his son: "You have never in your life finished anything you started and I don't believe you are going to start now. We gave you piano lessons, and you didn't practice. We bought you a Scout uniform, and you didn't go to meetings."

In every illustration presented in this chapter, gratification of a child's need or wish was denied by a parent. In each instance, inevitably the parent-imposed frustration produced some degree of anger in the child.

The reader could observe that in every case the parent was

acting to frustrate the child not because of some inherent meanness but on the basis of some virtuous, logical-sounding premise. It is the very virtuousness and rationality of their thinking that lull parents into believing they are acting in the child's best interests. And yet in each instance, inevitably the parent-imposed frustration produced some degree of anger in the child.

Problems with children arise because children are irrational. The logic of the parents' thinking is meaningless to children. All they know or feel is that they are frustrated and angry. The virtue of the parents' intent does nothing whatsoever to reduce the child's anger.

Parents must recognize that such well-intentioned hurting does not really help their children. As a matter of fact, such parent-imposed frustration is responsible for bringing about those very traits of behavior (i.e., selfishness, irresponsibility) which its application is supposed to prevent.

What happens is this: As the growing child becomes more and more angry with his parents, he becomes separated from them. Rejecting them as people, he rejects also their attitudes, values, and codes of conduct which he (being irrational) has experienced only as oppressive and alien forces. Now having rejected one group of standards, the child will need others to live by. It is only natural then that he will seek out values opposed to those of the parents. These he will find existing somewhere within the loosely affiliated, anti-middle-class, drug-oriented "rebel" subculture of our society.

Of course, I am not suggesting that parents who act in the manner of any of the illustrations given would produce inevitably a delinquent child. Probably all normal parents have acted toward their children, at times, in some of the ways described in these case illustrations. All parents must at various times deny some requests or block the satisfaction of some of the needs of their children.

I do suggest, however, that parents who act toward their children regularly and consistently in ways similar to those of the parents described in the case illustrations will in time create an unfavorable balance in the love bank. When the love has thus been drained and anger predominates, family conflict, delinquency, and drug dependency are likely to occur.

Use your own powers of deduction. What would you conclude from the following?

In the City of Los Angeles there exists a cult of Devil worshipers who have founded a church, complete with its own rituals. One of their prayers consists of saying the Lord's Prayer backward. Can you imagine how difficult it would be to learn this prayer backward? Would you surmise that their parents taught it to them backward? Or, would you guess that as children they learned it in the proper order and then later became "alienated" and as an expression of hostility reversed it?

And another fragment of evidence to consider: Patricia Krenwinkel, one of those convicted in the sadistic Tate–LaBianca murders, was quoted as follows in *Time* magazine, February 15, 1971:

"Squeaky described the tribe's radically unordered life: 'You could say it's a nonsense world of Alice in Wonderland, but it makes a lot of sense. Everybody makes their own rules. . . . Each moment is different.' "

Miss Krenwinkel, you will recall, "was a good baby, was never a behavior problem, . . . was gentle, sang in the church choir, went to summer Bible School, taught the Bible, liked religion, and was never hostile, violent, or disrespectful."

In the case of Patricia Krenwinkel, as in many others, the reader will find evidence of two factors: (1) genuine parental efforts to provide the child with wholesome, moral guidance, and (2) a young adult whose behavior reveals in most violent form the exact opposite.

This opposition, of course, is not accidental. An understanding of the relationship between these opposites would enable parents to take steps to see that it did not happen to their own children.

The message communicated to us by hostile, alienated youth is this: The indiscriminate, well-intentioned enforcement of rules and standards, every one of which independently is virtuous, logically defensible, essential to the growth of character, of modesty, of good grooming, of taste, of self-discipline, of chastity, etc., becomes oppressive enough en masse to make a child sick with rage.

In the illustrations given so far in this chapter, the parental decisions to block the satisfaction of the child's needs or requests were based on some rational consideration. I wish to describe now a specific class of parental actions that frustrate or block the satisfaction of a child's needs unrelated to any rational considerations whatsoever. These actions are dependent solely upon the momentary whim or impulse of the parent. I define this type of parental behavior as arbitrary. As I indicated previously, the child routinely experiences some degree of anger whenever he is denied gratification. Arbitrarily imposed frustration is even more detrimental to the child's welfare because quite regularly it produces instant rage. The result of persistent arbitrary treatment by the parent is a chronically enraged child for whom delinquency in some form is a virtual certainty.

Here follow several illustrations of arbitrarily imposed frustrations which the author has observed. As you read these various vignettes, try to imagine what you yourself would have felt if you had been in the child's position.

SITUATION: One Sunday afternoon an eighteen-year-old boy, who has just recently received his driver's license, asks his father for permission to drive the family car. The boy wants the car just for the fun of driving it, but he makes up as his "cover story" the pretext that he wants to go to the corner store to buy the family some ice cream.

The father is and has been reclining comfortably in front of the television set watching a football game, which is about one half completed. The mother is busy with some routine task in the kitchen. No one has any plans for using the car, which is parked in front of the home, that afternoon or that evening.

Nevertheless, the father refuses to give his son permission to use the car to go to the ice-cream store.

In denying the son's request, the father says: "You don't need the car to get ice cream. You can walk or take your bicycle."

What made the father's decision arbitrary is the fact that there existed no sensible, rational reason for denying the child the use of the car. The car remained parked on the street unused, all of that afternoon and evening, and the son knew it. The father simply did not wish to grant his son the pleasure of driving the car.

In most instances the arbitrariness of the father's decision to frustrate the child could be disguised or hidden completely. There is almost always at least one virtue to which the father could appeal in order to justify his decision, making it sound as if the frustration imposed was really in the child's best interest.

Typically, in such situations, a father might rationalize as follows to the son: "You are not the only person in this household. Don't be selfish. Someone else might want to use the car today"; or: "You don't care how you spend my money, do you? Well, I just can't have you driving all over town burning up gasoline that is being paid for with my hard-earned money"; or: "I can't have my son driving all over town unsupervised. That's the trouble with parents today. They let their kids drive anywhere they want; then they're surprised when the kids get themselves in trouble. Well, I'm not that kind of father."

But in cases of purely arbitrary decisions, such as this one, recourse even to such transparent arguments is not available to the father. Specifically in this case: (1) No one in the family had any need of the car that day. (2) The destination was so close to home that the cost of the gasoline to be consumed became a completely negligible factor. (3) The destination was very specific and did not involve giving the son freedom to drive "all over town."

Because these rationalizations are not available, the basic cruelty of the father's decision is clearly revealed to the child.

The child reacts, predictably, with rage. Wouldn't you?

Parents who indulge in such arbitrary actions, when questioned, will usually defend themselves in the following two ways:

1. The boy did not need the car in order to get to the ice-cream store. Nobody ever died from a brief walk.

2. I was acting within my rights. Since I own the car, I may give it to or withhold it from whomever I choose.

In routine conversations, these two arguments have enough "truth" in them to enable the parent to justify his actions.

The question I present to such parents, however, is this: Have you not lost sight of your primary goal? Is it your goal to choose intelligently among a wide range of possible parental actions those which seem most likely to enhance the parent-child relationship and thereby also the child's mental health? Or, is it your goal to act toward the child in ways that are thoughtless, unfeeling, or cruel, based on nothing more meaningful than past prejudice or momentary whim, and then to prove by the superior use of intellect that you have acted within your rights?

Often, the goal of the parent who frustrates his child arbitrarily has become diverted from that of doing what is best for the child to that of proving that what was done was proper or legal, in spite of the obviously detrimental effects on the child's welfare.

The eighteen-year-old boy of this case illustration was a chronic drug user in constant difficulty with the police.

Situation: The author observed the following events while having a cup of coffee one day in the outdoor eating area of a neighborhood restaurant. The eating area consisted of perhaps twelve tables, only three of which were occupied. It was almost two P.M. At one table sat a party consisting of two mothers, each with one boy approximately ten years of age. The two boys finished eating their sandwiches. The mothers continued intermittently eating and conversing.

One of the boys stood up quietly, walked over and sat down alone at a table in the sun, adjacent to the one at which his mother was sitting, which was in the shade.

As soon as the mother noticed his departure, she called out to him angrily, "What are you doing there?" The child replied, "It's cold over there." The mother became furious at this. "You come right back here!" she said, and began thrashing about in an agitated manner, probing deeply into a large shopping bag. She repeated aloud several times: "Where is that sweater? What did I do with that sweater?" Although she was not able to locate the sweater, she insisted, in her most commanding voice, that the boy "come over here right now and sit here by me."

The child complied quietly, and he then sat down in the shade next to his mother. The mother resumed her conversation, as before, with the other woman.

Again in this case, as with the first in this chapter illustrating arbitrarily imposed frustration, the rationalizations frequently used to disguise the inappropriate use of parental authority are lacking. The raw use of parental power, untempered by judgment or compassion, is clearly revealed to the child.

Clearly, in this instance there existed no sensible reason for the mother's refusal to permit her son to sit alone at a table in the sun. If the boy had been boisterous, the mother might have justified her own action by claiming that she was "only thinking of the rights of other adults in the coffee shop." However, the child had been sitting alone, quietly. If the child had occupied a table during the noontime rush hour, the mother could have justified her action on the grounds that "we must have consideration for some busy adults who may have an immediate need for a table." However, it was late in the afternoon and nine other tables were unoccupied. If the boy had not finished his sandwich, the mother might have insisted that she wanted the boy at her side solely in order that he eat "all that good, healthy food." But the boy had already consumed his entire sandwich. If the boy had chosen to sit at a table in the shade, the mother could have argued that she wanted him to sit near her in the sun so that he wouldn't catch cold. But she herself was seated in the shade, while he was seated in the sun.

The complete irrationality of the mother's action is revealed even more clearly by the fact that she insisted that the boy be seated next to her, in the shade, even though she was never able to find his sweater. There exists not one single "virtuous" reason that can be found to justify this mother's misuse of her parental authority.

The only "mistake" the child made was to have an independent thought and to initiate an independent action while in his mother's presence. The mother's exercise of authority was designed to demonstrate to the child that he was to subordinate himself to the mother's will at all times.

Sometimes, in desperation, a parent will attempt to justify such use of authority on the grounds that it is a good way to teach obedience for possible future use, even though admittedly the immediate demand itself is irrelevant.

One of my adult patients told me the following anecdote about his mother, who had tried to teach him as a child about the desirability of obedience to a mother's commands:

"I want you to learn to listen to me and to obey me instantly at all times. At first you will not understand why this is so important for you to do. But someday, for example, you could be walking along some railroad tracks. A train would be rushing up behind you but you would not hear it. I would see the train about to kill you and I would holler, 'Lie down!' Because you had trained yourself to obey my orders instantly, without thinking, you would fall down flat and the train would pass harmlessly over you."

I hope this mother's explanation makes clear how desperate and overpowering was her own need to assert total control over her son, not for his own welfare, but in order to satisfy her own need for dominance.

The growing child will experience this parental assertion of power as a threat to his emerging manhood and selfhood. Human nature is so constituted that he is bound to fight, in some way, for survival. Since the parent is striving so desperately to instill total obedience to authority (particularly his own), the natural tendency of the child will be to struggle for survival by fighting against authority, by becoming disobedient and disrespectful toward those in control.

13

THE CORRECT WAY
TO SAY "NO"

The two principles described in the preceding chapters (gratify the child's needs whenever possible, and never frustrate him arbitrarily) are designed to reduce irrational anger. This leaves unanswered, however, the question as to what can be done about the irrational anger generated when parents must necessarily block the gratification of their child's needs. At first it might appear that nothing can be done to reduce his anger in these situations, short of giving in to the child's requests. Surprisingly, perhaps, this is not the case. By a careful choice of words, parents can convey a particular attitude to the child, which is capable of reducing anger—even while blocking the gratification of the child's need or impulse. It is not essential for the parent to gratify each and every request of the child. However, it is very important for the parent to learn how to say "No" in such a way as to keep the child's anger to a minimum.

The mistake most commonly made by parents in such situations consists in choosing too carelessly the words they will use in denying the child's needs or requests. Usually, the words chosen inadvertently convey to the child the impression that the parents do not want to gratify him and that they would not gratify him even if they had the means for doing so.

The poor choice of words confuses the child concerning the parents' basic motivations. The child comes to believe that his parents do not want him to be happy, or even that they enjoy seeing him miserable. In the child's mind this translates very quickly into the idea that "they don't really love me." The result is anger and parent-child separation.

To guard against this misunderstanding, parents must learn to choose very carefully the words they will use when denying a child's requests. The words chosen should convey to the child the idea that the parent really desires to gratify the child in order to make him happy, even though the parent is unable to do so in some particular situation. The proper choice of words will convey to the child what is essential for him to know, that the parental actions toward him are motivated by love.

The case illustration immediately following is a classic example of situations in which parents routinely find themselves. A child makes a request which the parent must deny. Two versions of this incident are presented. The first illustrates how the situation might be handled by the average, frustrated parent. The result is excessive anger. The second describes how the situation should be handled in order to minimize anger. As you read about these two different approaches, try to empathize with the child's feelings in each. Then, decide for yourselves: (1) Which image of a parent would you want the child to hold of you? (2) Which way would you prefer to be treated if you were in the child's situation?

A mother is shopping one day in a full-line drugstore for routine household items. She expects to spend approximately three dollars in this store. Her five-year-old son, however, spies a large toy, prominently displayed, which carries a price tag of $17.95. He asks for the toy.

His mother replies, gently but firmly: "No. We're not here to buy toys today."

The child does not accept this answer and persists in asking for the toy. At times his voice becomes a "whine." The mother persists in refusing his request and gradually becomes more and more angry herself.

The child is unable to resist temptation and asks for the toy at least one time more than the mother can endure. Her anger reaches its first, minor peak. "Now look," she says menacingly, "I told you you're not getting the toy, and that's it! So you'd better stop bugging me!"

In his disappointment, the child deteriorates farther into irrationality and states the unforgivable, "You never buy me anything I want!"

The falseness of the accusation, together with the ingratitude revealed in the child's remark, acts as a catalyst that changes the mother's emotion from one of intense anger to almost uncontrollable rage. She begins to reprimand the child vehemently. Her jaw is rigid, with the teeth held very closely together to help her avoid shouting too loudly in the crowded store. Her eyes narrow. "You rotten, ungrateful little brat," she says. "You have more toys than any other child in the neighborhood. You have toys in the closet you don't even have time to play with."

At this point, if the mother feels sufficiently persecuted by the child, she might hit him. At the very least, however, she will assign a punishment to be put into effect when they return home from the shopping trip. This threat usually involves either a spanking or depriving the child of toys he already has, in order to "teach him proper appreciation." On the way home from the drugstore she refuses to speak to the child.

The primary emotions governing the parent-child relationship, as they leave the drugstore, are those of mutual distrust, disappointment, and anger.

This entire sequence of interaction was initiated by a simple request that the parent could not fulfill. Gradually it escalated to the point where the mother assaulted her child both verbally and physically. At the conclusion of the incident, not only had the child failed to receive the toy he wanted but in addition (temporarily, at least), he had lost his mother also. The result was a degree of anger far in excess of that which might have been generated had the child suffered solely the loss of the toy, while retaining the emotional closeness to the mother.

Adults will have no difficulty in recognizing that the mother's decision to withhold purchase of the toy was completely reasonable and that she loved her son even though she denied his request. We must wonder, however, whether or not the child will remain convinced of his mother's love after she: (1) declined to purchase the toy he wanted, (2) called him a rotten, ungrateful, little brat, (3) slapped him and threatened further punishment, and (4) refused to speak to him for a substantial period of time.

This situation can be dealt with far more benignly if mothers would just remember to use these two words, "I'm sorry," and be willing to use them over and over until the child gets "sick" of hearing them.

Using the same illustration again, suppose that after the child asked for the expensive toy the mother had initiated a dialogue with him that began with the statement: "Honey, I'm so sorry! I would love to buy you that toy, but it just costs too much money."

This statement is not designed for and should not be expected to make the child stop demanding the toy. He will persist in asking for it again and again. The mother's response is designed to create a particular feeling in the child toward the parent in spite of her continuing refusal to purchase the toy he wants.

Thus, the second, third, and fourth time the child requests the toy, the mother will just as insistently tell him how very sorry she is that she cannot buy it for him.

The dialogue might sound something like this:

CHILD: Oh, Mother. Look at that truck! I want that, Mother. Buy it for me.

PARENT: Oh, honey, I'm sorry. I just can't buy that for you now. It costs too much money.

CHILD: Oh, Mother. It's so big. I don't have a truck I can ride on. I want that one.

PARENT: Yes, I know dear. It is such a beautiful truck. I would love for you to ride on it and have lots of fun. But, I just can't buy it for you today. It's so expensive.

CHILD: (*Authoritatively*) I want that truck, Mother, and
            I'm going to take it home!
PARENT: Honey, I know how much you want that truck and I
            really would love for you to have it, but it just costs
            too much money. I can't. I'm sorry.
CHILD: Oh, you! You never buy me anything I want!
PARENT: Dear, I know you are very angry with me now and
            I'm so sorry I can't buy that truck for you. You tell
            me just as soon as you get over being angry with me.
            Okay?

Why is it necessary to say, "I'm sorry," when the child's request and accusation are both illogical and unjustified? Because
in so doing, the mother undermines the further development of
the irrational anger. Yelling, scolding, and punishing the child,
confronting him directly with the evidence of his own irrationality, serve only to help him justify the irrational anger.

By withholding rebuke, condemnation, and punishment the
mother also withheld from the child the "ammunition" he
needed to justify his irrational accusation. This makes it
possible for the initial anger generated by the denial of his request to dissipate more rapidly.

The child, of course, would remain disappointed and somewhat angry, because he didn't get what he wanted. However, his
anger would have to be far less intense than it might otherwise
have become if his mother had been abusive and assaultive toward him.

At the time the parent and the child left the drugstore the
child would still be angry, but only mildly so. The mother and
the child would remain on speaking terms and even the relatively mild anger would have been "softened" by the mother's
insistence that she was sorry she couldn't give him what he
wanted. She would have presented herself to the child as someone who loved him and wanted to make him happy, rather than
as the primary obstacle to his obtaining satisfaction in life.

The child was in no danger of becoming spoiled because the

mother remained firm and persisted in denying him what she believed she could not reasonably provide. Since he did not get what he wanted in this situation, and in many others of a similar nature, the mother was not guilty of "getting him everything he ever wanted."

What the mother did accomplish was to say "No" in such a way as to convince the child that she loved him, and thereby reduce his anger. This provided a basis for reconciliation after the mild anger passed and for continuing the closeness between the mother and the child. Of course, in order to do this, the mother had to accept the overt expression of a certain amount of anger and even an unjustified criticism.

This show of parental acceptance, understanding, and tolerance helps the child to discriminate between his parents, who love him, and the other impersonal mechanistic people or forces in society. It is this parental giving of something extra which builds the child's love and loyalty to the parents and to the parental values.

This approach, of course, demands a great deal of patience and self-control on the part of the parent. It is much simpler and more acceptable socially to yell at or even hit the child who is acting like a "pest." But I remind parents that these are the appropriate times to show such loving self-sacrifice. Years later, when the parental plea is being made, "Doctor, I'll do anything to get my child free of these poisonous drugs," the opportunities for constructive self-sacrifice may have passed.

The previous example illustrates only one means by which the mother could have reacted to the child's requests in order to reduce his anger. But there are available to parents several other courses of action that can serve to reduce even further the child's irrational anger. These involve attempts to offer partial or substitute gratification for the deprivation imposed. When used with sensitivity to the child's needs, the approach not only reduces irrational anger but produces love in its stead. At the very least, however, the utilization of any of the following techniques by the parent will always serve to reduce anger in those situations in which the parent is constrained to say "No" to a child's request.

Imagine again the situation in which the child has asked his mother to purchase the truck costing $17.95. Having decided to turn down his request, she might still respond with any of the following comments: (1) "I know what, let's put that truck on your birthday (or Christmas) list and then when it's your birthday, maybe Daddy and I can surprise you with it." (2) "I sure would like to buy you that truck, but it costs so much money. I'll tell you what! I will talk to Daddy tonight and we will see how long it would take us to save the money to buy it for you. You could save, too, and help us." (3) "That really is a beautiful toy, dear, but it costs so much money I just can't get it for you now. I'm so sorry! But, look, here is a nice little toy and it costs only 98 cents. Let's buy this one and maybe that will help you to feel better." (4) "Honey, I'm so sorry I can't buy you the truck you want today. I know how much children love toys like that. But this is what we'll do. When I'm through shopping, I'm going to get you an ice-cream cone [or, When we get home, I'll give you a glass of chocolate milk and a cookie . . . read you a story, etc.]."

The child might accept any one of these suggestions, in which case his anger would dissipate immediately. Or, he might prove implacable. But even if the child rejected all parental efforts at compromise and conciliation, the most damaging thing the parent would have said at any time would have been "Honey, I'm so sorry I can't buy you the toy you want today." This kind of statement does not build or sustain anger. Thus, the relatively mild anger generated by the parent's initial refusal would have to be minimal and transient. So, too, would be the degree of separation experienced in the mother-child relationship. But, on the other hand, if the child accepted any of the parent's suggestions, the mother and the child would find themselves united in a common cause, figuring out how to provide the gratification the child desired. The mother and the child would have something very exciting to talk and plan about. The child would be looking forward to greeting the father that night in order to see what his father could contribute toward the purchase of the truck.

If the child becomes convinced that his parents are motivated primarily by the desire to block the satisfaction of his needs, he will feel that they do not love him and he will respond in kind. On the other hand, if the child is convinced that his parents are motivated by the desire to help him attain happiness or pleasure, he will feel loved and will again respond in kind.

Children are more sensitive to the parental attitude toward pleasing them than they are to the actual cash value of the material goods received. Because of this, children of poverty-stricken parents may grow up with strong feelings of appreciation and of having been loved while the children of more affluent parents who received more capital goods may feel both deprived and unloved. The crucial factor is not how much the parent was able to give materially, but how effective the parent was in conveying to the child the attitude that she wanted to please him and to see him happy.

The following are several other examples of commonly occurring situations in which various of the approaches mentioned in this chapter could be used profitably by parents:

SITUATION: A six-year-old is having a birthday party. She has been the center of attention and received a great many privileges. But she demands still more. When the party games begin, she wants to be first in line, at all times, because she is "the birthday girl." The mother, however, insists that the child be the last in line because, "It is your party, and therefore you are the hostess."

The child insists that it is not fair that she be last. The mother becomes angry and rebukes her publicly with names such as "selfish, inconsiderate, ungrateful . . . and . . . a baby." When the child remains unhappy, the mother accuses her of "spoiling such a lovely party for all these nice children." Eventually, the child's unhappiness enrages the mother to the point that she warns: "I'm not going to do anything to you right now, but just wait until everyone has gone home! I'm going to set you straight, young lady, in a way you won't forget!"

The party began as a pleasant experience for the child. But, by the end of the afternoon, she was angry, frustrated, depressed, fearful of her mother, and separated from her.

The mother gave the party because she loved the child. And yet, because of her reaction to the child's irrationality, the child became aware not of parental love but of parental anger. The time, trouble, and expense of the party, which reflected the mother's good feelings toward the child, were completely wasted.

The mother should have handled the situation differently. When the child complained about the requirement that she be last in line, the mother should have said simply and sympathetically: "Dear, I'm so sorry. I know how difficult it is for a child to wait in line and especially when that child is the birthday girl."

If the child continued to pout, the mother would keep insisting that she was sorry. Eventually, the child would relent. The party situation would demand it. For example, ultimately, the birthday cake would have to be cut. The birthday child would have to cut and receive the first slice. At that point, if one did not arise sooner, the child's anger would dissipate. Moreover, because the parent had not magnified the problem, a very rapid reconciliation between the child and her mother would be possible.

At the end of this party the "scorecard" would read something like this: (1) Child did not get everything she wanted. (2) Child was unhappy or angry part of the time. (3) Child enjoyed herself most of the time. (4) Mother and child were very close and loving after the party.

SITUATION: A mother is at the checkout stand of the local supermarket. Her daughter, aged approximately three and one half, is at her side. While the mother is watching various items being rung up on the cash register, the child moves a few feet away from her and looks up, smiling, at the next person in line.

The child is wearing a one-piece jacket and hood combination, with a high, pointed top, tightly zippered and tied with a string at the neck. The mother notices, suddenly, that the child has stepped a few feet away from her. She grabs the pointed top of the child's hood, lifts the child off the floor in this manner and swings her "airborne" three or four feet back to the cash register.

The child immediately begins to cry. She repeats several times, "You choked me." The mother replies, "Well, you're gonna get choked a lot more if you don't learn to mind me."

The child continues to cry. She holds the mother tightly around the leg with both arms and buries her face in the mother's skirt. After a few minutes the child turns her face from the mother's skirt. The cashier, sympathetic to the child's plight, smiles at her and says, "You're getting to be a big girl, aren't you?" The mother volunteers sternly, "No, she's not and she'd better learn to mind me or she's going to regret it."

The term "ambivalence" is used often by psychologists. It means to hold mutually opposing or contradictory feelings toward the same person or object. The statement "I love him but I hate him" is an example of ambivalence.

If the reader wishes to understand the concept of ambivalence, he should try to empathize with the feelings of the child clinging to the leg of the mother, who, moments before, had assaulted and degraded her. In later years, this child's behavior will be determined by both the love and the anger she felt toward the mother. Because of this, the child's behavior might alternate between "good" and "bad." Or, at some point, if the anger came to predominate, the child's entire mode of personality functioning might shift suddenly toward delinquency. This is how ambivalence operates.

Many delinquent, drug-dependent young people are able to state openly that they do love their parents. These statements may be accepted as true. They are inaccurate, however, in that they omit reference to anger, the more powerful portion of their ambivalent feelings which is determining their actual behavior.

The question arises as to how significant a part of the child's development is the kind of incident that took place at the checkout stand of the supermarket. As I have stated previously, no single incident of this sort, nor even a series of such incidents over a period of years, can create sufficient anger to cause delinquency. As long as such events are relatively rare occurrences, as long as they constitute a very small portion of the totality of the parent-child interaction, they will effect no injury to the child's personality development.

It is only in those cases in which the mother's actions at the checkout stand reflect a consistent attitude toward child-rearing which would make such actions commonplace that the danger of delinquency will arise. It is the consistency of the parents' attitude that will generate repeated actions of frustration and unintended cruelty which, eventually, will enrage the child beyond the level of endurance.

There are several other ways in which the mother in the supermarket might have dealt with her daughter without running the risk of producing excessive anger: (1) She could have tried calling to the child gently, "Come over here by me, honey." If this had failed, the mother could have (2) taken the child gently but firmly by the wrist or by the sleeve of the coat and pulled her closer to herself. (3) If the child seemed inclined to wander away, the mother might have placed the child in the seat portion of the shopping cart provided for children. (4) Additionally, the mother could have spoken more kindly of the child. For example, after pulling the child back to the cash register area, the mother might have said something such as, "She really is a very good girl, but every once in a while she forgets to mind and I have to remind her."

None of these approaches would produce excessive anger or ambivalence.

SITUATION: A nine-year-old child must take medication regularly as prescribed by his doctor. The parents have purchased a large quantity of the medication in pill form. The child becomes very upset each evening because he finds that he "gags" as he attempts to swallow the pill. He whines, whimpers, complains, and cries, but his parents insist that he swallow the pill "like a man." They accuse him of being "a baby . . . of gagging just to make a scene . . . and of wanting to waste our money."

Each evening the child becomes more and more angry with his parents. Being irrational, he cannot comprehend that they are forcing him to swallow the pills in order to protect his health. They attempt to explain that they want him to learn to swallow pills without gagging because he will have to do so all his life. The child is aware only that he barely avoids suffocation every night and that his parents appear to be responsible for it.

The child's anger and his misunderstanding of the parents' motives could have been reduced significantly if the parents had done either of the following: (1) Ground up the pill and attempted to dilute it in a pleasant-tasting liquid. (2) Asked the physician, who prescribed the medication, if it was available in liquid form.

Here again, try to imagine how this child might have felt toward his mother or father if either one had said to him one evening: "Son, I'm so sorry. I know how difficult it is for children to swallow pills. I used to hate it myself. Tomorrow I will call the doctor and ask him if he can prescribe a medication that you could sip from a teaspoon."

Again, note that the basic request of the child was not met. That is, he still had to take his medicine. However, by expressing sympathy and attempting to reduce the discomfort involved, the parents presented themselves to the child as his ally and protector rather than as his own personal Torquemada.

SITUATION: During a shopping trip, a ten-year-old girl decides she wants a two-piece bathing suit she sees on display. The mother declines her request and informs the child: "I wouldn't buy anything like that for a girl who looks like a big fat pig. Look at those rolls of fat on you."

As the child returns home from the shopping trip, she is carrying three items: (1) a one-piece bathing suit, (2) an intense dislike of the mother, and (3) a feeling of humiliation.

How would you feel if you were the child? How would you feel toward your husband or wife if he or she spoke to you in this manner?

The very most the mother should have said in this situation if she was not going to purchase the two-piece suit was, "Oh, honey, I'm so sorry. I just don't think that would look good on you."

SITUATION: The author was to deliver a lecture at a junior high school one evening. He arrived at the school, which was unfamiliar to him, parked his car, and found that there was no ready way to identify the building that housed the auditorium. The campus was quite large and poorly lighted.

A young boy on a bicycle was passing nearby and the author asked directions from him. The youngster stopped and very politely gave directions. In addition, without being requested to do so, he began to guide the author directly to the auditorium. The boy would bicycle ahead, slowly, a few feet, then turn around, make certain his charge was still with him, and then proceed farther across the campus. In this manner the youngster led the author almost to the doors of the auditorium. He had done all he could, short of placing the visitor on the stage.

The author thanked the youngster, who started to pedal away. At that point a grounds keeper who had been working on the lawn nearby looked up and snarled at the child: "Hey, you! Get out of here with that bicycle. Beat it!"

I have often wondered what effect the grounds keeper's remark had on the child. Did it help him to feel more kindly or more trusting of adults? How might this young man be likely to respond the next time he came across an adult in need of help? Would he speak just as politely? Would he be as generous with his offer to help?

Parents are disappointed and puzzled when they find that young people talk of "not trusting anyone over twenty-five." "Where do they get such crazy ideas?" the parents ask. The answer is very simple. These feelings of animosity toward adults develop over the years as adults act harshly, insensitively, and disrespectfully toward children on the assumption that children are entitled to nothing more, or that kindness spoils them.

In response to this line of reasoning, adults are prone to defend themselves with the counterargument: "The grounds keeper was only doing his duty. It was his responsibility to see that bicycles were not permitted on campus."

To me, this argument is nothing more than a rationalization, an example of adult irrationality. It enables parents to evade direct confrontation with the harshness of their own actions toward children and of the necessity for change.

There do exist other ways in which the grounds keeper could have carried out his duties and fulfilled his responsibility that would not have involved his speaking arrogantly and disrespectfully to the child. For example, he might have waited in silence to see whether the child remained in the area or was merely passing by. Or, if the child remained, the grounds keeper might have said to him in a friendly manner, "Son, I'm sorry, but you know no bicycles are allowed in this area."

Only if the child were deliberately disobedient and refused to leave the scene would it have become necessary for the adult to speak more authoritatively to him.

Note that regardless of whether the adult ordered the child away with a harsh command and a snarl or asked him sympathetically to leave, the end result, in one respect, would have been the same. The child would have left. The rule would have been enforced. Adult authority would have been respected.

The results are different, however, in what the child feels inside himself as he leaves the scene. Under one condition he leaves with a feeling of injured pride and anger. Under the other, he leaves feeling reasonably comfortable. The feelings the child develops from this one incident with the grounds keeper, together with thousands of others from interaction with parents and other adults, will determine the child's attitude toward the adult world and the rules and regulations established by adults. These attitudes will then determine the child's behavior toward the "Establishment" in subsequent years.

The idea that the misunderstanding between generations is caused by a breakdown in communications is an adult fantasy. The breakdown is not in communication but in the adult's inability to respond sensitively to the child's feelings. Only different treatment of children by adults can correct the attitudes the children have formed toward the adults.

14

THE IMPORTANCE OF
HAVING FAITH IN THE CHILD

Many parents are aware of the important part that the concept of faith plays in their lives. Their own faith in God is both a source of comfort to them and an inspirational resource that helps them to establish and live up to moral beliefs in everyday life. Many parents are aware also, through familiarity with the New Testament, of how having faith in an imperfect individual can have a miraculous effect in strengthening his character. Many of these same parents, however, remain unaware that this same principle, faith, can play an equally constructive part in enhancing both the parent-child relationship and their own child's character. Whether or not the parent ever becomes aware of it, the issue of faith or the lack of it will arise between himself and his child. A great deal will depend on the manner in which parents deal with this matter. To the extent that the parent is able to manifest and maintain faith (or trust) in the child, he will enhance loving feelings and the growth of the child's conscience. However, to the extent that the parent demonstrates lack of faith, he will strengthen the irrational portion of the child's mind, create excessive hostility, and weaken the child's conscience. In these respects, the parents' withholding of trust in the child will have precisely the same impact as their administering excessive disapproval and punishment.

The following are a number of illustrations of commonly occurring points of parent-child interaction in which opportunities for demonstrating faith or lack of faith may arise. These may occur at almost any time in the child's life. In one of the examples given in this chapter, the child described is only three and one half years old. Note that in all the examples provided here the parent expresses a lack of faith in the basic goodness or decency of the child. The result, inevitably, is anger.

SITUATION: A nine-year-old child lives two blocks from the local school. On a corner midway between his home and the school is a small grocery store. Many of the neighborhood children stop at this store on the way home from school and buy ice cream or candy. The nine-year-old is not permitted to stop there but must come directly home. The mother fears that if she permits him free time to "just idle" on the way home from school, he will get into mischief.

In a similar situation, a thirteen-year-old boy is forbidden to ride his bicycle to a shopping center located two blocks from his high school to "just look around." He is given permission to bicycle to the center if he has a specific purchase to make and a specific destination. He is expected to return home promptly as soon as the purchase is made. One can almost hear a sepulchral voice whispering into the parents' ear, "The devil finds work for idle hands."

Contrary to what many parents expect and are taught to believe, it is these overly supervised children who tend to become disturbed or delinquent and not those who are given some degree of freedom of movement. The overly restricted child would have two reasons to be angry with the parent: (1) because a simple pleasure was denied him, and (2) because the parent demonstrated lack of faith in his character.

By their actions in restraining their children, the two mothers described here were communicating the following message to them: You are inherently evil. If I let you out of my sight, you will immediately manifest this evil in some form of misconduct. I, on the other hand, am good. Fortunately for you I have the power to control the evil impulses within you that strive constantly for expression. This, of course, is not said by the mothers in words. However, it is clearly stated in their restrictive actions.

This is a very satisfying position for the parents' ego. The mother retains possession of all the goodness in the situation and the child is awarded all the badness. But the child will resent the fact that all this badness is projected into him by the parent. He will feel that if his mother loved him, she should think more highly of him and trust him. He will interpret her lack of faith as a lack of love and he will respond accordingly. The mother's explanation to the child that she is merely fulfilling her parental responsibility will have no effect on reducing the child's feeling of having been betrayed by his own mother.

Very often the challenge to the parent to demonstrate faith occurs when the child acts impulsively or speaks irrationally. Here are several examples:

SITUATION: A nine-year-old boy is standing on the sidewalk in front of the house. He watches as his father arrives home from work and parks his car in the driveway. The boy whistles to his father in order to get his attention and to say "hello." The father becomes very angry and orders the child into the house for the remainder of that day. The child asks what he has done wrong. The irate father explains. "Nobody whistles at me. I'm not a dog."

The father's lack of faith here was shown in his misperception of the child's motives. The father assumed that the child was attempting to humiliate him and not simply attempting to greet him. Obviously this child is going to react with feelings of hurt and anger. Reciprocating the father's distrust, the child now trusts the parent less than he did previously. He will not reach out toward his father quite so openly on the next occasion they meet.

SITUATION: An eight-year-old girl comes into the kitchen and finds her mother putting some cookies into a small plastic container. The child suggests, cheerfully, that the mother put the cookies into a larger glass jar, shaped like a squirrel. The mother becomes very defensive and irritated. She yells at the child: "Don't you get smart-alecky with me, young lady. I know very well how to put cookies away without any help from you."

Here again, as in the previous example, the parent misjudged the child's motives. The mother assumed that the child was assaulting her intelligence and reacted violently in order to defend her own integrity. The result unfortunately is that the child and the parent grow farther and farther apart as each such incident takes place. Would you imagine that after thirteen or more years of this type of interaction the child would consider this mother a sympathetic and interested listener, the first person to turn to for advice and comfort with teen-age problems?

If this mother had any trust in the child's basic decency, she might have said to the child, simply, "Thank you, honey, that's a fine idea," or "Thank you, dear, that's a good idea, but your squirrel won't fit in the drawer and this little box will."

SITUATION: At the conclusion of some minor conflict an angry five-year-old child yells at his mother, "Sometimes I just hate you, Mommy." The mother is greatly offended at this and yells back at the child: "Well, if you hate me so much, you can just get out of this house and find yourself another mother who will cook for you and feed you and take care of you. And as long as you hate me so much, don't come around begging me to give you dinner later."

If the mother had understood her child well enough, she would have known that her five-year-old was not basically evil, monstrously ungrateful, and consumed with hatred. She would have realized that he was just frustrated and angry because he did not get something he wanted; and that children, being irrational, tend to make wild or exaggerated statements in order to express their momentary feelings. If she had been able to trust the child, she would have realized that he still loved his mother but that he was very angry with her at the moment. On the basis of her own faith, then, the mother would have been able to speak to the child in a more reassuring way, which would have laid the groundwork for rapid reconciliation. She might have said, for example: "It's all right, Son, I understand that you are very angry with me right now. And I'm angry with you too. I don't like it when you yell at me. But we'll be friends again soon. You'll see."

SITUATION: One evening a father takes his eleven-year-old son and one of the boy's companions to a movie. One scene of the movie depicts a rather pathetic event where a small deer is caught and eaten by a crocodile. The boy's friend is properly horrified at the blood and destruction, but the son jokes and laughs uproariously at what is happening to the small deer.

The father, suspecting that his son is some form of monster, responds with self-righteous rage. He begins to assault the boy vigorously in front of the other child. He calls the son "stupid," "insensitive," "callous," and "sadistic" and says that he is ashamed of the son. The father concludes his lecture by vowing that he will never take his son to another movie as long as they both shall live.

The father in this situation demonstrated his lack of faith in his son by accepting the jocular behavior "at face value." The father reacted as if he had suddenly discovered evidence of the child's evil nature, which previously the boy had been able to hide. The violent verbal assault by the father was designed, as it always has been, to drive the evil spirit out of the child. But note that implicit in the father's rage and disapproval as the child experiences them is the idea that there is some innate badness in the child that must be driven out by the morally superior adult.

The child, by his own actions at the movie, had initiated the father's anger and reprimand. Nevertheless, the son will feel betrayed by the father, who could not understand that "deep down" the son was good and not evil. In response to the parental rejection and the public humiliation he will become less trusting and less loving toward the father. Six months later, this same father might ask a friend quite innocently: "Why is it that kids don't like to go places with their parents? They seem to like to go only with kids their own age."

The outcome could have been entirely different if the father had been able to mobilize some trust in his son. During the eleven years of the child's lifetime, the father should have had many opportunities for observing that his son had the capacity, at times, to be kind, generous, understanding, and sympathetic. During the movie, then, rather than condemning the child for one transgression from perfect morality, the father could have reassured himself concerning the basic decency of the son. Having thus reassured himself, the father would then have been in a good position to reassure the child. Thus, for example, in response to the son's silliness the father might have said gently to the friend: "Don't pay any attention to what he's saying now. I'll bet that inside himself he's just as upset at seeing that deer killed as you and I."

This reassurance is a statement of faith in the child. It communicates to the child the idea that the father understands him better than anyone else in the world. It comforts the child himself who may have secret doubts about his own normalcy. This expression of faith is a completely loving gesture on the part of the parent. The child experiences it as such and responds in kind. After statements of this sort the parent and the child become closer than ever before. A child treated this way has less reason to shun his parents as many teen-agers so commonly do.

SITUATION: One evening at the dinner table a seventeen-year-old announces to his parents his discovery that "Cops are pigs." The parents are horrified at this radical development in the teen-ager's personality and initiate vigorous argument in defense of policemen, on the need for law and order, etc. The parents point out (quite correctly) that policemen perform a vital function in a civilized society. These logical arguments, however, have no effect on the teen-ager, who argues back vigorously (and irrationally) until tempers flare. In desperation the father resorts to the use of his parental authority. "As long as you are living under my roof and eating at my table you will respect the authority of the police. I will not have you making statements like that. You may leave the table this instant. Your company is not welcome until you have changed your views."

What is the result of this well-intentioned effort by the parents? The teen-ager is now more angry and antiauthoritarian in his attitude than ever. For him to admit of any virtue in a police officer would represent a humiliating capitulation to the greater wisdom and power of the parents. Maintaining an attitude of hostility toward the police has now become an important part of the teen-ager's feelings of independence and masculine pride. All possibilities for dialogue with the parents have been cut off. The child has been given two choices. Either capitulate to the parents' way of thinking or get out.

But suppose now that the father had been able to maintain some faith in the son's character. He might then have interpreted the son's statement about "pigs" as a minor transgression in an otherwise fine young person, a typical manifestation of the "folly of youth." If the father had been able to do this, he would not have become so angry with the son. He would not have felt it necessary to mobilize all the power vested in the parent to reprimand, to punish, etc., in order to stifle the developing evil in the boy once and for all.

If the father was not so self-righteously angry, he might have spoken to the son more as an equal. In this case, the father could have said something like this: "Well, Son, I guess I can see how young people today might not like policemen too well. I guess the kids don't like being told to get off the beach at night or to stop making too much noise, and things like that. I'll tell you the truth, Son, I still get mad at policemen myself whenever I get a ticket even when I know I'm dead wrong. But you know, when I get calmed down and think about it I realize someone has to do what they're doing." Note that in the father's statement he shows some understanding for the child's position but still does not condone the child's use of the phrase "Cops are pigs." The father grants that the child's character is probably not much different from his own. This kind of statement leaves open the possibility for further parent-child dialogue. It does not increase the child's hostility toward either the father or the police. At the conclusion of the meal, the parents and the boy are still friends. Perhaps the son feels even closer to his father because the father admitted to being human himself rather than casting himself in the role of the perfect adult with the defective son. Certainly the son will not have been driven even closer to the radical group that generated the "Cops are pigs" philosophy. This is the value of love expressed through faith.

Many parent-child conflicts that center around the concept of faith are related to the child's (particularly the female's) sexual development. Such conflicts may occur at almost any age, but are usually most numerous just prior to and during the teen-age years. Parents, routinely, interpret their daughters' activities in this area as premature and attempt to assert a restraining force. Fashions and customs change. But whatever the current fashion, if it suggests sexual maturity, the parent would prefer that the child "wait a little longer. There's time enough for that sort of thing later." Thus, the average parent will insist that the child delay for one or more years wearing makeup, wearing clothing that reveals the female figure, dating boys, etc. The parental fear underlying these delaying tactics is that permitting the child to grow up too soon will lead rapidly to a pattern of sexual promiscuity. Many parents have explained their position as follows: "If I let her wear eye shadow at thirteen, what in the world will she be doing for excitement at sixteen?"

The following are examples of commonly occurring situations in which the parents' fear of the child's sexuality leads to serious misunderstanding between the child and the parents.

SITUATION: A girl three and one half years old is standing at the curb talking and giggling with a little boy the same age who lives across the street. Suddenly she lifts her skirt so as to hide her face, and her underpants become exposed. The girl's father, witnessing the scene from inside the house, rushes out, pulls down the child's skirt, spanks her, and drags her into the house. He warns the child: "Don't you ever do that again. That's dirty."

How will an incident like this affect the child's feelings toward her father, toward men, and toward her own body? Will a routine pelvic examination by her physician cause her severe embarrassment later? Will she be capable of enjoying sexual intimacy with her own husband?

SITUATION: A fourteen-year-old girl hangs a large colorful poster in her bedroom. The poster displays prominently the face of a young singer of whom the parents disapprove because of some question about his morals. The parents inform the daughter of their displeasure with the singer and request that she take down the poster. The daughter insists that she wants the poster to remain. Finally, after the child refuses a direct order to remove the poster, the mother enters the child's bedroom and tears it down herself. The mother explains that the prominent display of the face of a man of questionable morals is a threat to the morals of the entire family.

SITUATION: One evening a sixteen-year-old boy and girl are seated in the family room of the girl's home. This room adjoins the living room in which the parents are seated watching television. Large double doors between the two rooms are open. Sometime during the evening the daughter closes the double doors that separate the two rooms. On seeing this, both parents jump up immediately and reopen the doors. They look very reproachfully at both young people. The mother informs them that it is "not proper" for two young people to be alone in a room where they cannot be supervised.

Other parents in corresponding situations have expressed similar sentiments and have asserted their authority to prevent boy-girl contacts. In one case a mother refused her daughter permission to study and do homework at a boy's home because it was not "proper," even though the boy's parents were to be in the house at all times. Another father became acutely disturbed when he found a teen-age boy sitting at a desk in the daughter's bedroom helping her with her homework.

SITUATION: A fourteen-year-old girl returns home from school at three fifteen P.M. daily. She is not permitted to enter the house, however, until the mother returns home from work at five thirty in the evening. The mother explains her reasoning as follows: "If she got into that house before I did, she'd just have a bunch of boys in there with her. It wouldn't be too long before she would get herself pregnant. But even without that, it wouldn't do her reputation with the neighbors much good if they saw her in the house alone with boys all the time." When asked whether the daughter might not get herself in just as much "trouble" at some remote location outside the home, the mother replies: "Well, at least then I've done my duty and it's not my fault. But if I let her use her own home to do it, then it looks like I'm condoning it and I'm just as much at fault as she is."

The reader could observe that in each case presented here the parents revealed a lack of faith in the child's basic goodness. Instead, in every instance there was the presumption of evil within the child that would assert itself the moment the parents relaxed their ceaseless vigil. Although the parents may not wish to do so, this persistent display of parental distrust communicates to the child the idea that they view her as no different and no better than a tramp. In their single-minded dedication to protecting the child against her own lustful appetites, many well-meaning parents remain unaware of the extent to which they are hurting the child's feelings.

This lack of faith, demonstrated repeatedly by the parents, drives the child toward sexual misconduct in at least two different ways. First, it makes the child very angry, because she feels betrayed by the parents' lack of confidence in her. Since it is irrational, the child's anger then demands some form of revenge against the people she feels have hurt her so deeply. The most obvious means of vengeance available to the child is to do exactly the opposite of the parental wishes. Secondly, the falseness of the parental accusations stimulates the child's irrational behavior to new heights of activity and undermines rather effectively any possible restraining effect of the child's conscience. Many young women reason (irrationally) as follows: "Well, as long as my parents think I'm a tramp and keep accusing me of being a tramp, I might as well act like one and at least get some of the enjoyment out of it." These are the underlying forces which account for the fact that so many teen-age girls from well-run, carefully supervised, middle-class homes produce such a large number of "problem pregnancies" or participate in impulsive, premature marriages that have little, if any, chance for success. Approximately one million children ran away from their homes last year. The majority of these were white girls from middle-class families. Would you imagine that these girls were running away from homes in which they had received an overabundance of warmth, respect, and trust?

Parents, of course, have the right and the responsibility to teach their children socially desirable codes of conduct. But it is not sufficient merely to teach moral values without taking into account the child's feelings and his irrational thought processes. What many parents do not as yet understand is that the moral education of the child is taking place, not only when the parents are lecturing, scolding, moralizing, supervising, and punishing but whenever the parents are acting in any way that affects favorably the balance existing between love and anger within the child.

The really important issue in the child's moral development is not what the parents can make the child do while she is located inside the home, directly under parental supervision. What is important is how the child behaves when completely free of direct supervision by an authority. When moral values are taught "coldly," unaccompanied by loving actions such as trust, the results will be anger and rebellion against the values being taught. Conversely, when moral values are taught by a parent who manifests love through maintaining faith in the basic goodness of his own child, the result will be a return of love and an acceptance of the values being taught.

The ancient Hebrews well understood this principle. The following anecdote concerning one Aaron the Good appears in traditional Jewish writings: "Aaron was the great peacemaker in Rabbinic legend. He would, in the case of an open rupture between two men, hasten first to one, then to the other, saying to each: 'If thou didst but know how he with whom thou hast quarreled regrets his hard words to thee!' with the result that the former enemies would in their hearts forgive each other. . . . His kindness led many a man who was about to commit a sin, to say to himself, 'How shall I be able to lift my eyes up to Aaron's face!' Thus did Aaron turn away many from iniquity." [3]

Aaron's goodness acted to strengthen the conscience of another individual. In its strengthened condition the conscience was able to guard against the expression of bad impulses. Like Aaron, modern-day parents must be willing to use their own goodness as the instrument that will help their children to develop a healthy measure of self-control. When the child looks into the parent's eyes he must see someone there who resembles Aaron the Good or Jesus. Parents can reveal their love by having the courage to maintain faith or trust in the basic decency of their own children.

To see how faith operates in everyday situations let us consider the case of the teen-age girl, referred to in this chapter, whose parents insisted she leave the family room doors open in order that they be able to watch her. Suppose that after school on the following day she met a group of boys who were experimenting with marijuana. They explain to her its joys and virtues and ask her to join them. If you take just one "hit," they tell her, no one can ever smell it on your breath. Do you imagine that this girl would respond immediately by thinking to herself: Oh, my. These must be just the kind of boys Mother and Dad have been warning me about. I must be very good and go right home! No. It is far more likely that this girl would join in the "fun" and enjoy it even more deeply because she knew that she was doing secretly what the parents most feared and despised.

But what if the parents had acted differently? Suppose they had been able to manifest their trust in the daughter by allowing her to remain behind closed doors with a boy. By refraining from opening the doors, the parents would have been communicating an important message to the child, nonverbally: You are our daughter. We know you, we love you, and we trust you.

You behave correctly because you are basically a good person and not solely because you fear what we might do or say to you. Suppose that at the end of the evening the mother was able to say to her daughter something like this: "I guess I can still remember what it's like to be at that age when young people enjoy being alone, with no grown-ups around to bother them."

A child treated in this way responds with love, not anger. When this child is presented with temptation on the way home from school, she is not likely to say to herself: "I think I'll just try some 'grass.' That should shake up the old bitch." She is far more likely to reason: "How could I ever face Mother? She is so good to me. This would break her heart." This is the manner in which faith asserts its healing power.

There is no way, of course, that a growing child who is consistently imperfect can earn the kind of faith I am asking parents to show. From the beginning the child will be narcissistic and do nothing but take, take, take, while the parent gives. Then, being irrational, he will make mistakes repeatedly. He will be chronically imperfect and fail to live up to the highly moral standards of the parent. Yet who on earth, if not the parents, will be capable of giving so freely, in love, what the child cannot possibly earn but still needs so desperately?

As I have indicated previously, human nature is so constructed that one feels a profound sense of appreciation toward another human being who has offered kindness. It creates a feeling of obligation to return something of value to the individual from whom one has received something freely given. Faith is a major portion of the kindness that parents can offer. And if it is offered generously, the child will repay the obligation by growing up to be reasonably happy and a productive member of a civilized society.

REFERENCES

1. Benjamin Spock, *Dr. Spock Talks with Mothers* (Fawcett Publications, Inc., 1961).

2. Marguerite and Willard Beecher, *Parents on the Run* (Grosset & Dunlap, Inc., 1967).

3. Joseph H. Hertz, *Sayings of the Fathers* (Behrman House, Inc., 1945).